YOU
CAN
DO
IT!

Lewis E. Losoncy is Professor of Psychology at Reading Area Community College and Director of the Institute for Personal and Organizational Development, Reading, Pennsylvania. An international lecturer in the areas of encouragement, communication, and positive attitude, he is also the author of *Turning People On* (Spectrum Books, Prentice-Hall).

YOU CAN DO IT!

How to Encourage Yourself

Lewis E. Losoncy

Foreword by Albert Ellis

A SPECTRUM BOOK

PRENTICE-HALL, INC. Englewood Cliffs, N.J. 07632

Library of Congress Cataloging in Publication Data

LOSONCY, LEWIS E
  You can do it!

  (A Spectrum Book)
  Bibliography: p.
  1. Success. 2. Courage. 3. Self-respect.
I. Title.
BF637.S8L594   158'.1   79-19033
ISBN 0-13-976605-7
ISBN 0-13-976597-2 (pbk.)

Editorial/production supervision and
  interior design by Carol Smith
Cover design by Peter Ross
Front cover photograph by Nestor Corteijo
Manufacturing buyer: Cathie Lenard

A SPECTRUM BOOK

10 9 8 7 6

Printed in the United States of America

PRENTICE-HALL INTERNATIONAL, INC., *London*
PRENTICE-HALL OF AUSTRALIA PTY. LIMITED, *Sydney*
PRENTICE-HALL OF CANADA, LTD., *Toronto*
PRENTICE-HALL OF INDIA PRIVATE LIMITED, *New Delhi*
PRENTICE-HALL OF JAPAN, INC., *Tokyo*
PRENTICE-HALL OF SOUTHEAST ASIA PTE. LTD., *Singapore*
WHITEHALL BOOKS LIMITED, *Wellington, New Zealand*

In respectful memory of
Dr. Alfred Adler,
who put people in their place—
in charge of their life;
his voice grows stronger each year.

And to the rare and courageous person
who lives Adler's ideas
and takes full responsibility
for life.

Contents

Foreword

It seems as if thousands of self-help books keep plummeting from the presses every year and that few of them are particularly original or worth reading. Most of them seem to hark back to old schools of thought that never had much validity in the first place and that have even less today—such as the profound mystical claptrap of the Oriental thinkers and the recondite overgeneralizations of the psychoanalysts. But, as that great psychologist of the nineteenth century, P. T. Barnum, sagely said, "A sucker is born every minute!" And the widespread sales of some modern self-help manuals bear him out with a vengeance.

Not so in the case of Dr. Lew Losoncy and his book, *You Can Do It!: How to Encourage Yourself.* First of all, he starts with one of the oldest, most readable, and clearest of the mental health models: that of the ancient Stoics and of their leading teachers, Epictetus and Marcus Aurelius. Some two thousand years ago, following the teachings of Zeno and other Stoics who lived some six hundred years before his time, Epictetus wrote in *The Enchiridion*, "Humans are disturbed not by things, but by the views which they take of them." This phenomenological outlook, which is at the basis of several of the leading schools of modern psychotherapy—especially Alfred Adler's individual psychology, George Kelly's fixed role therapy, and my own rational-emotive therapy (RET)—is the one taken by Dr. Losoncy; and he applies it beautifully to the principles and practice of do-it-yourself therapy outlined in this book.

As stated by the author in Chapter 3: "Much discouragement is a result of two basic mistaken beliefs about self, others, and life. The first error is in the failure of people to face and accept reality as it is. The second major mistake is in the failure of people to realize all the possible alternatives available to them once they face and accept that reality." Well put! If, as I have stated in various of my writings, people would only recognize that whatever is, is and that there is never a reason why it *must* be otherwise, they would rarely disturb themselves about practically anything. And if they would secondly realize that once they accept reality and choose a certain path or goal as desirable, there is no reason why they *must* stick only to that choice and ignore many other possible alternatives, they would not stay disturbed for very long. For almost all human problems, however deep and long lasting, have *some* solution, and the art of living largely consisting of giving up absolutist commanding, insisting, and *must*urbating and adopting, instead, a reasonable attitude toward accepting one or more of the existing possibilities.

Humans, however, do not live either by bread or philosophy alone. As much as I have espoused, for the last quarter of a century, perhaps the most cognitive or philosophic method of psychotherapy among the many existing schools, I have always tried to weld cognition closely with emotion and action. Consequently, RET is very consciously and determinedly a form of cognitive–emotive–behavioral therapy. Dr. Losoncy, to my own great liking, has followed a similar rule and has incorporated into *You Can Do It* a variety of self-help methods that are, first, highly thoughtful; second, distinctly emotive and evocative; and third, extremely active-directive. Although his own philosophy is one of democratic tolerance of other people's foibles and fallibilities, he is nicely intolerant of inefficiency. He has, therefore, at almost every step of the way, included direct, clear-cut, practical applications of cognitive restructuring, showing the reader exactly how to force—and I mean *force!*—him- or herself to fight against and act against habitual sloppy thinking and dysfunctional behaving.

Blame or intolerance is one of the main essences of human disturbance. Dr. Losoncy accurately distinguishes four different types of blame: group blame (e.g., the Russians, Society, the Americans); other-person blame (e.g., "He hit me first!"); thing blame (e.g., "This weather makes me miserable"); and self-blame (e.g., "Because I did a rotten thing, I am a rotten person!"). Showing people that they have these kinds of intolerance, and that they thereby may make themselves temporarily feel good (as when they are angry at others) but that they later make conditions worse (as when these others get angry back at them), is an almost necessary part of effective psychotherapy. But this is not enough: The therapist then is called upon to devise means of helping clients to surrender their damning of themselves, of others, and of things and to practice nondamning attitudes and actions over and over until they automatically and "unconsciously" take over.

This book has many exercises that at least partially take the place of a therapist. I cannot guarantee that profound personality change will automatically ensue for anyone who follows these exercises and keeps practicing many of them over and over. But the raw material of change is in these pages. And I can guess, with at least a high probability of success, that any reader who seriously imbibes the rational messages of this book and who forthrightly and steadily works on many of its precise exercises will have an exciting cognitive adventure, will bring about some dramatic emotive changes, and will habitually function better than before glancing at its pages. No book of a self-help nature is a panacea for emotional ills. But this one can at least provide a head start toward healthier and happier living.

Albert Ellis, Ph.D.
Institute for Rational-Emotive Therapy
45 East 65th Street
New York, NY 10021

Preface

Take a few moments to think of some of the most courageous moments of your life. Perhaps there were times when you courageously overcame nearly insurmountable odds to reach a long-desired goal. Or maybe major adjustments in your life, such as a new job, loss of a loved one, or marriage, called for you to energize your courage. Or perhaps there were times when you courageously trusted yourself and stood up for what you believed even though it was not the popular thing to do.

How much courage do you have? *You are at least as courageous as your most courageous moments.* We believe that this kind of courage exists within you all the time, waiting to be energized to assist you in reaching your life goals. That's what courage is—the willingness to change and to move toward your goals in life—both an attitude and a skill. We also believe that like a muscle, you can develop your inner courage with practice and come to a full understanding of yourself and your potential courage.

If you are like most people, however, you use only a small

portion of your inner strengths. The truly courageous person is a rare phenomenon, which is not surprising if you consider all the "invitations" in life to become discouraged and lose trust in yourself. Have you ever experienced any of these invitations? Did other people—parents, teachers, bosses, etc.—ever tend to

- notice your negative points and weaknesses and ignore your strengths and resources?
- dominate you by telling you how you should feel and even what you should believe?
- compare you with other people, inviting you to feel okay only when you won?
- accept you only when you did the "right thing" or were perfect or did well by their (not your) standards?

Or are you your own worst enemy? Did you ever invite yourself to become discouraged? Do you ever tell yourself

- I'm afraid to try new things because I know I'll fail.
- I can't stand it when somebody criticizes me—I either fly off the handle or just sit back timidly while I seethe inside.
- Things just aren't fair—other people I know can eat all the cakes and pies they want and don't gain a pound, and I just look at food and gain weight.
- If only I were born into a different set of circumstances, I could. . . .
- I'm so afraid of getting older.

These are just some of the many invitations for you to lose courage and give up your sense of adventure for living. We call these "invitations" rather than "causes" because we believe that discouragement is ultimately your choice. Yes, with every invitation there is an RSVP, and you have the option of replying either "yes, I will become discouraged" or "no, I will not become discouraged—instead, I am going to become more determined."

If you are like most people, you will live approximately 25,600 days. Anything is possible for you in just one of those days. Ask yourself what you want. Each day can represent potential newness, excitement, and movement toward your goals, packed with all the excitement that life and other people have to offer; or you can feel that one day is just the same as another and that life is just a process of "getting by." Today can be just another day or the beginning of the dream of the future. Thirty years from now you might look back and say, "If only I could go back, I would really change my life and enjoy it more fully," or you can make today the dream of the future by taking advantage of the fact that you are here and alive.

You Can Do It! has been written to invite to you energize your inner courage by recognizing the powers and resources that you have available within yourself. Chapters 1 and 2 focus on recognizing and dealing with invitations for you to become discouraged. Chapter 3 discusses the philosophy of realistic positivism, a productive and courageous way of looking at your life. Chapter 4 demonstrates ways of developing your identity, self-respect, personal resources, and enthusiasm. Chapter 5 focuses on ways of speaking courageously to yourself by eliminating self-defeating words from your vocabulary. Chapter 6 shows ways of bravely overcoming discouraging beliefs about yourself, other people, and the world. Finally, Chapter 7 puts it all together to invite you to achieve the dreams of your life.

Permission has graciously been granted to reprint material from Turning People On by Lewis E. Losoncy (Englewood Cliffs, N.J., Prentice-Hall, 1977 and *Humanistic Psychotherapy* by Albert Ellis (New York, McGraw-Hill, 1974).

When you have finished reading, we hope you believe that life is to be enjoyed and that anything is possible.

You + Your Inner Courage = Anything

Yes, with the full understanding and use of your courage, you can attack any barrier, overcome any self-defeating attitude. You can face your only enemy in life—yourself—and move your strong foot forward, taking your first step toward everything you have ever wanted. *You can become one of the rare courageous people.* You need no longer look to other people to find out how worthwhile you are or how to live your life. You need no longer timidly accept what you believe to be your lot of life—instead of owning a lot, you can own the world. After all, you—and no one else—determine how you look at the world, and in the end that is what determines your outlook on life.

An Unproductive Way of Understanding Yourself

CHAPTER **1**

P erhaps you have been taught (that in itself didn't hurt you) and you believed (now *that* is what hurt you) that you are the way you are today because of external factors—your society, your parents, your church, your brothers and sisters, your teachers, your successes and failures, your physical appearance, and so forth. Comments similar to the following illustrate this kind of thinking and are accepted by many people to be explanations of behavior:

GEORGE, 22

I have a real problem with my anger. At times I fly off the handle and do things like slap my little daughter in the face. I know that it has brought me trouble with the courts, but you see, I do this *because of the way I was raised.* My parents always used physical force to control me, and so it was only natural that I would act this way.

JOHN, 25

I never dated much *because of my weight problem.* I am not very appealing to girls. I have always been so self-conscious that I thought if I asked somebody out, she would reject me—so why try!

George blames his lack of control today on his parents' treatment of him years ago. After all, he believes, it makes sense that since his parents abused him, he naturally would abuse his child. By accepting this, if we want to find the cause of George's actions, we should look to his parents. But there is a distorted sense of logic here: If George's parents "caused" his lack of control, do they not deserve the same excuse? We would have to concede that his grandparents were responsible for his parents' behavior, and so on, and so on. And it is impossible to get all these people in our counseling office to help George with his problem.

John's excuses include his physical appearance and lack of confidence caused by feelings of inferiority. If only he could look more attractive, he thinks, life could be a ball. But he is destined to live out his one lifetime in an unfulfilled helplessness.

"Fringe Benefits" of the Unproductive View

George and John have adopted the unproductive and discouraging view of explaining why they act the way they do. Why is it unproductive? Mainly because it stops them from taking charge of their lives and living each of their 25,600 days more fully. George is in trouble with the courts for child abuse; when his lawyer cites statistics showing that parents who abuse their children *tend* to have been abused themselves as children, George has an excuse for his actions. John's view is unproductive because he has never had the full experience of dating and he buys the belief that there is no hope for him.

Despite the fact that discouraging people think themselves into misery and unproductivity, they do receive many fringe benefits for the price they pay. What an ingenious way they have devised to protect themselves and avoid change in their lives! They are, in a sense, *passive* people. The cause for their behavior, they believe, is someone or something other than themselves. They are just helplessly waiting for external factors to shape their lives, some of which are illustrated below.

Psychologists often refer to the belief that one's behavior is *automatically* caused by past experiences or biology or any factor other than personal choice as S→R psychology. The stimulus (S) (e.g., your parents' abusive behavior) automatically produces your behavior, or the response (R) (e.g., your abusive behavior). This viewpoint suggests that you go through life with little choice in changing and controlling your actions. A stimulus, then, such as someone's calling you an unpleasant name, would *automatically* produce a response in you—for example, feeling hurt.

People who accept this explanation for themselves can easily be recognized by their language—it also is passive. When they speak, they place themselves helplessly following the verb or action part of their sentences. Thus, their behavior is not an action for which they are responsible but just a helpless reaction to someone or something else. For example:

> Mom really made *(verb)* me *(helplessly)* angry today when she yelled at me.
> Janet caused *(verb)* me *(helplessly)* to cry when she told me that she wouldn't see me anymore.

Notice the automatic response and helpless feeling expressed in each case. These passive sentences suggest that the cause for the speakers' helplessness was someone else who "acted on" the victim. Consequently, where does the blame lie for these persons' misery? Naturally—with the person who supposedly caused that misery.

Here is another example of a passive sentence:

> My boss gave me a headache today.

When this passive sentence is changed to an active sentence, it appears this way:

> I gave myself a headache by the way I chose to react to my boss today.

Changing a passive sentence to an active sentence takes the *blame* for people's decisions and (re)actions away from the external factors and places the *responsibility* where it belongs—with themselves.

Write two passive sentences, and change the sentences to an active form:

PASSIVE   ACTIVE

1. _____   1. _____

   _____   _____

   _____   _____

PASSIVE	ACTIVE
2. _____	2. _____
_____	_____
_____	_____

In passive sentences, the blame for people's decisions lies external to them. Who are these blame receivers?

Blame Receivers

The unproductive way of understanding the causes for your feelings, thoughts, and actions is to conclude that they were caused by someone or something other than yourself. These alleged causes are the blame receivers. At least four different types of blame receivers can be distinguished. These four are *group blame* (e.g., the Russians, Society, the Americans); *other-person blame* (e.g., "He hit me first"); *thing blame* (e.g., "This weather makes me miserable"); and *self-blame* (e.g., "I feel good every time I feel badly about myself" or "I am such a rotten person, I could never change"). Think of some blame receivers that you might include in each of these categories.

GROUP BLAME

Group blame (also known as Archie Bunkerizing) allows people the privilege of explaining their feelings, thoughts, and actions through the actions, real or imagined, of someone else. It serves the purpose of placing the responsibility for one's behavior on some nebulous quantity that, in most cases, cannot even be isolated.

9

EXAMPLE 1

The Democrats are responsible for my present economic situation.

EXAMPLE 2

Society makes me sick. Look at all the violence and rotten things happening today. In my generation we wouldn't have put up with it. It's these spoiled kids today.

In Example 2, the complainer is hard pressed to find and stomp down the culprit (Society) in his misery. Where shall this person write to get back at his nemesis? What is Society's address? Note again the passive language in the comment:

Society makes *(verb)* me *(personal reference)* sick.

How much time and valuable human energy are wasted in complaining about things that have a low probability of changing? Just look again at Examples 1 and 2.

EXAMPLE 3

My teachers had me frightened to death to go to school, and they made me quit when I was 16.

Example 3, of group blame, suggests that the reason that this student did not learn and consequently quit school was her teachers. Again, observe the helplessness of the person as demonstrated by the passive language. According to her, her quitting was a *direct result*, not of her decision, but rather of the actions and fear tactics of others. It should be remembered that although her excuse may perfectly well explain her decision in the past, it no longer is appropriate when she becomes aware of her responsibility to herself.

Jot in some examples of your own to demonstrate group blame:

_____

_____

_____

OTHER-PERSON BLAME

Children learn at a very early age that if they are accused of something, the way to save face (or skin) is to point the finger elsewhere. In these cases, the "scapegoat hunters" are again searching for reasons outside themselves to explain why they felt, thought, or acted as they did. Look at the dialogue in the following example.

EXAMPLE 1

Billy's Mother: Why did you hit Johnny?

Billy: He called me a name.

Johnny: Sure, I called you a name, but it was because you threw the baseball at me.

Billy: I did that because you called my Mom a name.

Billy's Mother (defensively): Oh, what name did you call me, Johnny?

How many times have you seen *blame-shifting* dialogues similar to this one? Many a mother, father, or teacher has been through this blame volleyball. Each person hopes to get the last word in and point the final finger. Where it all stops, nobody knows. How much valuable human courage and energy are spent wastefully in defense rather than growth?

EXAMPLE 2

Jim: Mary Ann rejected me—so I took the overdose.

In Example 2, the reason for Jim's overdose is not Jim but rather Mary Ann. Other-person blame is extremely effective in the short range. After all, is it not logical to conclude that the event was too much for Jim and that the overdose was an automatic result? Consider: Were there not any other alternatives available to Jim?

Mary Ann is the culprit or cause in this example. At this point, of course, Mary Ann is under a great deal of pressure to be a little phony and perhaps to deny her true feelings. It may even go to the point of Jim and Mary Ann's getting married, despite the fact that she is no longer interested in him. But perhaps she would rather be unhappily married than to be labeled the cause of Jim's potential suicide.

Include some examples of your own to demonstrate other-person blame:

_____

_____

_____

THING BLAME

In thing blame, the responsibility for your unhappiness, depression, immobilization, or anger is placed on an object, a quality or condition, or a rule. It is very effective in helping us avoid the blame-shifting phenomenon. After all, *things* rarely fight back. Can you picture it if they did?

EXAMPLE 1

Driver: This traffic makes *(verb)* me *(passive personal reference)* angry.

EXAMPLE 2

Basketball Player: I missed that shot because I tripped on the water on the floor.

EXAMPLE 3

If only I didn't have this inferiority complex *(a thing)*, I think I could be quite popular.

In Examples 1 through 3, the people believe they were done in by a thing—a bunch of cars, water on a floor, and the ultimate explanation of much immobility, the inferiority complex.

Include some examples of your own to demonstrate thing blame:

_____

_____

_____

SELF-BLAME

Self-blamers put the blame for their behavior on themselves as opposed to holding themselves responsible. When people take the *blame* for their behavior, this is just as unproductive as placing the blame on external factors. Blame is a moral judgment and tends to lead to negative personal evaluation but no change. We believe that taking *responsibility* rather than self-blame is productive. When people take personal responsibility, they *act* courageously and are not *immobilized*. But self-blamers are so filled with blame, guilt, worry, shame, and doubt that they use all their energies blaming themselves and have no energies left to get out of their self-created ruts. So, whereas self-blame results in self-pity, personal responsibility results in action and change.

Self-blamers have a real luxury. After all, if they feel guilty, they don't have to change. Surely just feeling guilty should be

14

suffering enough, they reason. Should they feel weak, someone strong will surely come along and take care of them and tell them they are okay.

The illustration that follows shows the difference between a self-blamer and a self-responsible, courageous person in a somewhat unfortunate, common situation.

The self-blamer wallows in rejection. He feels that his worth has been attacked, and he chooses immobility. The self-responsible, courageous person is concerned about increasing his skills—he has learned from the situation. He is using his energies to develop a more constructive plan rather than to swim in self-defeating emotions. He is active and responsible. Our self-blamer friend is passive and irresponsible. Both of them appear later.

Give a few examples that demonstrate self-blaming:

_____

_____

_____

The unproductive way of viewing why you are the way you are today is to put the responsibility for your feelings, thoughts, and actions outside of yourself or to put blame, but not responsibility, on yourself. This is the "blaming process." Some of the advantages of this blaming process have been discussed. Allow us to explore in more detail the paychecks or rewards people get when they become skilled at scapegoating or blaming. We call this the "temporary gaining process," since blaming affords people the opportunity to enhance themselves falsely or to shift responsibility, sometimes providing them with *temporary* gains.

Gaining through Blaming

"Most of the time people blame, for the moment they gain" is a tried and true fact. Avoiding responsibility for personal actions enables them to go back to childhood, when they had much less responsibility. In the safety of youth, they need not face reciprocal and responsible social relationships, job pressures, budgeting problems, etc. All they have to do is keep their noses relatively clean around the house and keep the finger pointing in different directions when they do things like knocking over antique vases. At that point, they are going through the training for adult scapegoating, or blaming others. They find that they will receive paychecks (attention, control, or avoidance of responsibility) just by constantly providing excuses. On the playground, they find that by saying the sun was in their eyes, they have an acceptable explanation for dropping the ball. In high school, their choice of isolation from others may be easily understood as being caused by a weight problem. But look at the paycheck. If they are too heavy, they can use that as a perfect excuse to avoid involvement with people. Imagine the dangers of losing weight—without it, they would have to face going out there into the unsafe, unkind world, which is full of potential rejections. Observe a few of the many ways in which people can fool themselves and experience temporary false gains.

GAINING THROUGH DEPRESSION

This phenomenon is quite frequently seen in episodes similar to this one:

College Student: I'm seriously considering dropping out of school.

Counselor: Can you tell me more about it?

College Student: Yes, you see this depression hit me lately, and I have missed a lot of classes because it forced me to stay in bed.

Counselor: How had your classes been going before this depression?

College Student: Well, I'm on academic probation now, and I need a C average this term that I suspect I'll never get.

This dialogue, played over many times in counseling offices, displays all the ingredients of the self-blame phenomenon previously discussed. The student assumed that the depression was the cause for her current behavior. The idea that "it forced me to stay in bed" was a logical explanation to her. She has shrewdly but unknowingly justified her current thoughts of quitting school by blaming them on the depression. The counselor, with further exploration, found that there were other problems present. Yet these problems—for example, poor academic performance—were not even suggested by the student. This made it impossible for her to cope responsibly. Notice the paycheck: My feelings have nothing to do with me; rather, they are the result of my psychological state. To whom shall she write to change her emotional state? Can you imagine this one!

People who create their depressions (yes, that's right—in many cases, the cause or enhancement of depression is the sufferer) receive many fringe benefits. Take a look at some of these fringe benefits:

1. temporary removal of responsibility

2. pity, sympathy from others

3. immobilization of self and sometimes of others who witness the suffering

4. getting back at others who want to go out but now have to stay home.

Add any additional fringe benefits of depression you can think of:

5. _____

6. _____

7. _____

These are some of the many reasons why behavior is so hard to change. Created symptoms provide rich temporary gains. Symptoms such as depression can be manipulative; they can give people control and get people off the hook. But most importantly, symptoms stifle and prevent people from growing and coping with the challenge of life.

GAINING THROUGH PASSIVE-AGGRESSIVENESS

Consider the following dialogue:

Wife: What shall we do tonight?

Husband: I don't care. You make the decision. *(hidden thought: I don't want to be responsible.)*

Wife: Are you sure?

Husband: Yes, anything is fine with me.

Wife: Okay. Let's go to the movie.

Husband (after the movie): That was boring.

The *passive-aggression game* (also known as the You-Make-the-Decision-So-I-Can-Criticize-It Syndrome) is very effective. Put the responsibility for the decision on someone else, so that they can be criticized for the poor choice they make. The personal gain is that the "manipulator" takes no responsibility if the decision turns out to be a bad one.

GAINING THROUGH INADEQUACY

The more adequate people are, the more likely they are to receive responsibility. John, an excellent handyman around the house, is frequently called on to assist everyone in the neighborhood.

By the same token, the more inadequate people appear, the less likely it is that they will be given responsibility by others. The self-blamer finds that appearing inadequate will provoke some strong rescuer to arrive to take responsibility.

EXAMPLE 1

Susie (age 6): Mom, I can't tie my shoes—it's just too hard. I'm too stupid!

Mom: Okay, Susie, I'll tie them now, but next time you try.

EXAMPLE 2

Hostess: I can't make lasagna for the party. My lasagna always tastes too spicy. Can you help?

Rescuer: Sure.

Though giving the appearance of helping the self-blamer, the rescuer rewards feelings of inadequacy. In Example 1, Mom is really communicating, "I agree with you, Susie—you are too stupid, and the next time you need help in completing something, you must turn to others."

Example 2 shows a rescuer who could have encouraged the hostess to develop responsible behaviors. Instead, she communicates (perhaps out of her own need or pity for the hostess) that she believes there is no hope of improving the lasagna-making ability of the hostess.

OBSERVING YOUR FEELINGS, THOUGHTS, AND ACTIONS

We trust that at this point, you are developing an increased sensitivity to "fringe benefits" of blaming. Consider the following feelings, thoughts, and actions, and jot in a few comments as to the possible temporary rewards of each:

FEELINGS

Anger: _____

Hurt: _____

THOUGHTS

People are no good—they will take advantage of you.

_____

Everybody cheats on their income tax.

_____

ACTIONS

Temper tantrums: _____

Violent behavior: _____

   The unproductive way of looking at your actions, feelings, and thoughts is to look "outside yourself" to explain them. Pushing the responsibility elsewhere enables you to feel adequate and safe for a period of time and to avoid changing. Using self-blame, at first glance, appears to be productive but might result, on the contrary, in feelings of inadequacy and self-pity and consequently, in giving up.

   Take a moment to think about the major concepts of Chapter 1. Consider the following questions.

Brush Up: Chapter 1

1. What major theme did you take from Chapter 1?

2. How can your irresponsible feelings, thoughts, and actions have temporary fringe benefits?

3. What is the meaning of S → R psychology?

4. Who or what are the four types of blame receivers? Give an example of each.

5. What is the difference between self-blame and self-responsibility?

6. Why is it usually productive, in the short run, to blame?

7. Why is it unproductive, in the long run, to blame?

8. How does speaking in passive sentences assist you in dodging personal responsibility?

9. Identify a time recently when you have used blame shifting. How could you approach this situation more courageously?

10. Why is the courageous, responsible person rare?

11. With what parts of this chapter did you disagree? Why?

12. What can you take from this chapter and use in your life?

Develop a plan for personal growth and courage to change something about your life. Jot in below:

_____

_____

_____

_____

A Courageous Way of Understanding Yourself

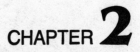

CHAPTER 2

The unproductive way of understanding your feelings, thoughts, and actions is to start with reasons that lie outside yourself. The more responsible and courageous way is to recognize that your emotions, decisions, and behavior are created and generated ultimately by you. You are in the driver's seat of your life. You choose your goals; you develop the most appropriate maps to reach those destinations; and it is you who can generate that exhilarating feeling of mastery when you move enthusiastically toward your goals.

When you adopt the blaming or complaining viewpoint of life, you orchestrate your own negative attitude and become hopelessly devoted to the safety of inaction. You are your own worst enemy. You may feel short-range comfort, but you are denying yourself the feeling of being alive—with no boundaries, no limitations—in each of your 25,600 days. As the systematic process of self-encouragement unfolds in the upcoming chapters, we trust that you will begin to feel more in control of your life than you ever dreamed possible. Can you ever give yourself a greater gift than this?

Finding and energizing this universe of courage and possibilities within yourself does not come easily. It takes hard work for which *only you* can be responsible. Part of the reason why change is difficult is that human beings are so complex. As a result of this complexity, we have decided to focus on the development of different aspects of you independently. We do believe, however, that you function as a whole, complete person, so that changes in any aspect of the self will affect you totally. So, in the final action chapter, we encourage you to "put it all together."

The philosophy of realistic positivism is addressed first. It is of the utmost importance to develop a realistic and positive way of looking at your life and at all your possibilities. Next, your relationship with yourself is discussed, since ultimately it is your beliefs and feelings about yourself that "invite" you to live courageously. Albert Ellis (1962) and Charles Zastrow (1979) have pointed out that what you tell yourself affects your emotional life; Chapter 5 is devoted to helping you develop a positive and more courageous language. Chapter 6 discusses ways of overcoming discouraging fictions that tend to immobilize you. Fictions about yourself, other people, and the world are addressed. Thus, in the end, we believe that the "proof is in the putting it all together." The chapter on courageous actions puts you, language, feelings, thoughts, and behavior together in a whole new brave and responsible you.

Many exercises, questions, and assignments are provided in each chapter to assist you in reaching your destinations. We share with you, as we have with many other people, the hopes, dreams, pains, and joys that you will experience along the road to energizing your inner courage. Have a lot of fun on your travels to a fuller life, and keep in mind the words of Buzz O'Connell, a master of encouragement, who contends that "life is too important to take seriously."

Moving toward Self-Encouragement

Now, we believe it is important to answer a few questions that are frequently asked about self-encouragement.

QUESTION 1: CAN PEOPLE REALLY CHANGE?

Perhaps you are skeptical about the possibilities of changing major aspects of your life after years of habit. We would not be surprised, because most people (who were totally honest with us) did not believe that they had the courage within themselves ever to achieve their dreams. But people *can* really change.

Through many hours of discussion and counseling sessions with children, adults, teachers, supervisors, corporation executives, and people from all walks of life (including "hopeless cases"), we have observed this movement progress from the "I can't," or the unproductive, viewpoint to the belief that "I am going to change." We have tried to isolate what we observed in the growth of these people. We have combined our observations with the writings and experiences of Alfred Adler, Albert Ellis, Carl Rogers, William Glasser, Rollo May, and many other contributors to a fuller understanding of the process of self-encouragement.

QUESTION 2: WHAT DO YOU MEAN BY "COURAGE"?

We believe that courage is the *willingness to change.* Totally sense that statement for a few moments. Feel it, think it. That phrase is the theme and goal of this whole book. We believe that anything becomes possible once you develop your courage, or willingness to change. Look at it this way:

$$You + Your\ Inner\ Courage = Anything$$

You have seen many traces of this courage in your lifetime. We believe that *you are at least as courageous as the most courageous moment in your life!* The chart on page 30 demonstrates what we believe best illustrates courage.

You might consider using this chart as a measuring stick as you take on the challenge of bringing out your inner courage. At the extreme left is the helpless attitude of "I can't." As you generate your courage, you will find yourself moving into more responsible, growing, and exciting directions.

COURAGE DIRECTION CHART

Courage Is Movement Toward →

"TURNED-OFF"			"TURNED-ON"
I can't make an effort.	I won't make an effort.	I can make an effort.	I will and am making an effort to change.
Constricted	Responsible but no movement	Responsible, hope, possibilities of movement	Constructive
Desire for mastery of sameness		Attitude growth	Desire for mastery of newness (courage of imperfection)
Stagnated			Growing
Nonresponsible			Responsible
Helpless			Effective
Opinionated			Flexible

That movement and its emotion are illustrated by the words in some of these songs:

- "I'm Ready to Take a Chance Again"—Barry Manilow
- "Let Me Try Again"—Frank Sinatra
- "Haven't Got Time for the Pain"—Carly Simon

The goal, then, is to develop the courageous attitude: "I will and am making an effort to change."

So we believe that courage is the willingness to change, to move toward new feelings, attitudes, or behaviors. We agree with Powers and Hahn (1978) that sometimes this movement can even be toward acceptance in instances where an individual refuses to accept inevitability. That involves much courage. We detail this point in Chapter 3—on the philosophy of realistic positivism.

QUESTION 3: WHAT IS THE PRODUCTIVE WAY
OF UNDERSTANDING MYSELF?

We believe that you can best generate your inner courage by understanding yourself through the blueprint first developed by Alfred Adler and later detailed by Rudolf Dreikurs. We urge you to consider carefully these three guidelines to a better understanding of "what makes you tick."

- Assumption I.   You create and determine all your feelings, thoughts, and actions.

- Assumption II.   All your feelings, thoughts, and actions are pulled by your goals.

- Assumption III.   It is the way you look at your life—not the way your life is—that ultimately affects you.

ASSUMPTION I

You create and determine all your feelings, thoughts, and actions. The unproductive way of viewing yourself is to blame your present-day feelings, thoughts, and actions on your past environment, your heredity, or other "external" factors. Blaming is quite common, and this, of course, is not surprising. As we have already discussed, there are many fringe benefits associated with placing the responsibility for one's life elsewhere. To make things worse, many behavioral scientists have encouraged this "reactive," "passive," and "helpless" picture of human beings.

Bill, age forty, was frightened of women. Although he wished to ask them out on dates, he lost his courage whenever the opportunity presented itself. In counseling, Bill disclosed that the cause of his fear was his mother, who used to dominate him as a child. He concluded that he consequently viewed women as strong and was frightened of them. He became so interested in his problem that he read a number of books on that subject and made copies of those pages that supported his position. He brought these articles to the counselor, pointing out that the research showed that domineering mothers tend to produce sons with problems similar to his. Thus, with this evidence, his anger at his mother as well as his lonely nights continued!

Bill's counselor pointed out that blaming his mother was illogical. After all, if his mother automatically made him be the way he was, then he couldn't get angry at her—because she has the right to the same excuse. If he is a direct product of his mother, so was she a direct product of hers. Thus, her domineering behavior was not caused by her but by her mother, and so on and so on.

The counselor also indicated to Bill that not all domineering mothers produce sons who have fears of women. There are many sons who had dominating mothers who are not afraid of women today.

The counselor then asked Bill, "Can you think of any fringe benefits in taking the blaming attitude?" Bill thought for a while, then replied, "Yes. I guess that I don't have to ask anyone out and can go on with my life of blaming."

The counselor discussed with Bill the fact that it would perhaps be more difficult for him to overcome his fear of women than for some other people who perhaps had less domineering mothers. However, Bill's first step was to take full responsibility, to realize that he had created his fears in the past to protect himself and that it was his choice and responsibility to become self-determined to overcome a perceived difficult past.

Pessimistic notions that people are doomed by their early experiences and that they change very slowly are giving way to the more encouraging ideas detailed by Alfred Adler over fifty years ago. Adler suggested that neither heredity nor environment is the ultimate determiner of personality, that they provide only the building blocks out of which we construct the person we want to be.

This again is not to deny the influence of genetics and envi-

ronment on you—each certainly is important. However, genetics
and environment are *just* the building blocks, and *you*, in the end,
arrange these blocks into the self-structure you want.

You are not just "reacting" to life—you are "acting" as well.
You create the stage to which other people react. Consider these two
youngsters:

> Beverly, age two, is always smiling and friendly. When
> relatives come to her house, she runs over to them, and as her
> eyes brighten up, she extends her arms and says, "I love you."
> Obviously, relatives love being with Beverly. The warm feed-
> back that Beverly gets from other people encourages her to feel
> that she is likable. She is developing a belief that the world is a
> nice place to be, and her confidence level with people is in-
> creasing.

> Louise, also age two, is constantly crying and fighting and
> refuses to let anyone pick her up. She is a whiner and is always
> unpleasant. When relatives come to her house, they tend to
> avoid her because of the way she acts. Louise gives a message
> to other people that she doesn't like them. They, in turn,
> respond by avoiding her. The feedback that Louise receives is
> that she is unlikable and that the world is a miserable, un-
> friendly place. So her negative behaviors snowball, and the
> cycle continues.

Even at two years of age, both girls are "setting a stage" to
which other people respond. *Yes, each girl is choosing to set the stage
to which others will choose to respond.*

Whose choice—Beverly's or Louise's—do you believe, in the
long run, will be more productive in securing harmonious human
relationships?

At some point in her life, we believe that Louise—by eliminating her blaming and by becoming determined to break this vicious
cycle—can change. A change on her part will invite others around
her to change. But she is responsible to start. Where else might we
expect changes in her life to begin?

We suggest then that your beliefs about yourself and your self-determination play the major role in whether you reach your goals or not. Consider this example from *Turning People On* (Losoncy, 1977). John and Bob approach an interview for a sales position:

> Confident John approaches a job interview with an attitude that says, "I can do the job and your company can profit from my abilities." The potential employer feels positive about John. (S)he feels John is capable of taking on the responsibilities of the position. John is hired and this gives him even more confidence.
>
> Bob, lacking confidence, meekly goes to a job interview with the feeling, "I'll never get this job anyway." He is apologetic throughout the interview and limits his responses to unsure yes or no answers. The employer reads Bob as a person incapable of assuming the responsibilities of the position. Bob never hears from the company again and this bears out his conviction that he is not worthwhile. His confidence is lowered and his next presentation of himself will be even poorer. [p. 25]

Can you remember times when you were like John? What happened?

_____

_____

_____

Can you remember times when you were like Bob? What happened?

_____

_____

_____

How could you have acted differently in these instances?

_____

_____

_____

Your beliefs are the key determiners of your successes and failures. *So create your expectations, and call forth your determination and courage.* Dinkmeyer (1977) wrote:

> Through our action or inaction, we are the determiners of our own successes and failures. We often get what we expect, even though we don't like to accept responsibility for our role as a potent force in determining what happens to us. However, through the influence of our expectations, intentions, and interpretations, we perceive experiences from a private logic. This private logic is the self-centered, biased private sense as opposed to common sense. These expectations influence the actual experience and, more important, our subjective experience of a situation.
>
> The person who goes to a party expecting to be bored will find the party boring. The person who anticipates that others will accept him or her usually finds acceptance. But why? Our attitudes and beliefs are manifested in our appearance, communication, and interpretation of life. The persons we relate with observe and interpret our nonverbal communications—a smile, frown, furtive look, grin, or nervous twitch. This influences the message they receive and the way they decide to interact with us.

Thus, we see the importance of the self-fulfilling prophecy in your successes and failures. If *you* don't believe in yourself and *you* don't become determined to reach your goals in your only lifetime—*who will?*

ASSUMPTION II

All your feelings, thoughts, and actions are pulled by your goals. When you take full responsibility for your life, you become responsible for everything that you feel, think, and do. This is contrary to the view that you can explain your behavior as being caused by external events or factors.

Courageous people believe that their behavior is not a reaction to external factors but rather an action to achieve future goals. Behavior, then, is not only caused but is also a cause in itself. Your feelings, thoughts, and actions are caused by you; they have a purpose—and this purpose is to reach your goals. Your behavior is constantly in operation—even when you are sleeping. Your behavior works, not by being "pushed" by your past experiences but rather by being "pulled" by a future goal.

We believe, then, that your behavior is best explained by viewing its results and goals. We don't ask, "What made you do that?" Rather, we ask, "What did you want to achieve by that action?" Look for the goal in this six-year-old boy's behavior:

> Johnny sees a toy that he wants at a store. He asks his mother if she will buy him the toy, and she says no. Johnny starts to scream, holds his breath, and eventually throws a temper tantrum. Johnny's mother is embarrassed by his display and buys him the toy.

What might have been Johnny's goal?

_____

_____

_____

If you suggested that his goal was to get power or to get the toy, we would agree with you. We don't believe that it is necessary to explain Johnny's behavior by relating it to some early childhood factors. Neither do we think that Johnny's behavior was necessarily driven by overwhelming forces that overtook him. We think that the explanation is simpler. We believe that his behavior can be best understood as being pulled by his goal—to get power or to get the toy.

Thus we have a great deal of trust in people. We believe that they determine and have control over how they feel, think, and act. We also believe that everything they do has a purpose and is directed toward a goal. To more effectively understand yourself, then, consider—not what you think causes your behavior—but rather what the results and paychecks are for your behavior.

Have you ever moped around the house feeling sorry for yourself? Perhaps everyone else ignored you. Did you get angry because they didn't give you sympathy? If so, perhaps your behavior at that time was directed toward receiving sympathy. We believe that this is a more accurate explanation than saying your behavior was caused by something that made you mope helplessly around the house.

Did you ever have an argument with someone and then lock yourself in your bedroom, kicking the door and screaming? Perhaps you felt "out of control." What would have happened if everyone had left the house and no one was there to get angry, feel hurt, or give in to your display? You probably would have stopped, since your behavior was no longer serving a purpose.

Observe children on the playground when they fall off a swing or a bicycle. The first thing they do many times is to see if anyone else is there to take care of their hurt. If no one is present, they continue on their merry way.

So we believe that it is more effective to realize that you create your feelings, thoughts, and actions to achieve an end result. That's the good news!

Now, the bad news. Although you are the executive of all your feelings, thoughts, and actions, most of the time you fail to make your goals clear. And when you fail to develop clear goals, other unrealized goals may take over. Remember that your feelings, thoughts, and actions are constantly being pulled by either your stated goals or your unrealized goals.

Unrealized goals are a talented and formidable opponent to you. Short-term satisfaction is one example of an unrealized goal that can snatch your employees (your feelings, thoughts, and actions) right from under you! Consider Ethel, whose *stated* goal is to lose weight. Observe the struggle between her unrealized goal and her stated goal as she is confronted with a high-calorie ice cream cake just after she has finished a big meal.

UNREALIZED GOAL	STATED GOAL
I want this ice cream cake now.	I want to lose weight.
FEELINGS:	FEELINGS:
It makes me so angry. Why do I have to be so heavy? It just isn't fair.	I feel so good that I can walk away from this ice cream cake.
It's so depressing when I look in a mirror. Well, I'm so bad off, what more will a little ice cream cake hurt?	And if I think I feel good now, just think how good I'll feel if I lose those ten pounds because of sacrifices like these.
Add some feelings of your own that lead to justifying eating the cake:	Add some feelings of your own that lead to losing weight:
_____	_____
_____	_____
_____	_____

THINKING

It shouldn't be this hard to diet. Just this one time won't hurt.

It's unfair. My sister can eat all she wants, and I just look at food and I gain weight. Heck, I'm not going to deprive myself of this food.

I deserve this ice cream cake. Look how hard I worked all week.

I'll start my diet tomorrow instead.

Add some thoughts of your own:

_____

_____

_____

ACTIONS:
Ethel eats the ice cream cake, and the unrealized goal wins out.

THINKING

It's difficult to turn this down, but I can stand it.

My sister is fortunate, because she can eat all she wants— that has nothing to do with me, however.

I might deserve the cake—it would taste good for about five minutes. But then I have to live with its effects. It isn't worth it and directly interferes with my goals.

I have control now, and it won't be any easier tomorrow.

Add some rational thoughts of your own:

_____

_____

_____

ACTIONS:
Ethel walks away from the ice cream cake, the stated goal wins out.

Identify some unrealized goals in your past that have generally won the battle. Remember, you as a human being are so powerful that you decide the winner. Successful people are those who direct their feelings, thoughts, and actions toward their stated goals. They state their goal, know their resources, and mobilize their feelings, thoughts, and actions into the desired direction, and they defeat their unrealized goals.

Courageous people take advantage of the constant pulling power of their positive goals. Life for them is the process of moving toward those goals. Goals are discussed at length in Chapter 7. Besides understanding self-determination and the purpose of behavior, another way of understanding yourself is to recognize the power you have in the way you look at life.

ASSUMPTION III

It is the way you look at your life—not the way your life is— that affects you. Discouraged people feel helplessly handcuffed to the events of their lives. They believe that they are the victims of fate, luck, or overpowering others. They also believe that there is only one way of viewing and responding to those events.

Courageous people, on the other hand, are aware of the powers of their personal perceptions of life. They believe that their happiness and growth are related to those perceptions. Thus, what happens to them doesn't affect them. What does affect them is the viewpoint they take toward occurrences in their lives.

Viewpoint of Life
(Perceiving Style)

Epictetus, the Stoic philosopher, said of life: "Nothing is either good or bad in itself—only thinking makes it be so." Epictetus was suggesting that the events of life only take on meaning when a human perceiver personally experiences and interprets them. This is the power of personal perception. The following examples demonstrate the importance of personal perception. Imagine how two people with these contrasting preceiving styles might differ in the way they react to the statement that follows.

STAN	STEVE
It's a dog-eat-dog world.	Life is okay. I'm glad to be alive and have an opportunity to enjoy life.
People will take everything they can get from you.	People are generally fair if you go halfway with them.
If people are nice to you, it's because they want something.	If people are nice to me, I go out of my way to show how much I appreciate it.

Get into Stan's perceiving style (viewpoint of life). Read the statement, and imagine that you see it as Stan would, considering his viewpoint.

STATEMENT
I really like your ideas. You are a real inspiration to me.

How might Stan view the statement?

_____

_____

_____

Now look at the perceiving styles chart, and imagine how Steve would look at the statement. Jot in some ways that Steve might see it:

_____

_____

_____

Compare your versions of Stan's and Steve's perceptions of the same statement. Did your responses suggest that they responded differently? If so, you've experienced Assumption III: You are not affected by what happens to you; rather, you are affected by the viewpoint you take toward what happens.

To demonstrate perceiver style, consider how adults often speak figuratively, and children hear the words literally. Just imagine how a young child perceives the following statements.

> EXAMPLE 1
>
> *Four-year-old Martha:* Mommy, where's daddy?
>
> *Mother:* Oh, he's tied up at the office.
>
> *Martha (in panic):* Oh, no! *(Pictures her daddy all tied up to his desk and gagged.)*
>
> *Mother:* Crazy kid.

> EXAMPLE 2
>
> *Two-year-old Jimmy:* Mommy, where's my brother?
>
> *Mother:* Oh, he's spending time in Turkey.
>
> *(Can you imagine Jimmy's perception of this one?)*

Yes, we are influenced, not by the facts, but rather by our perceptions of the facts—and they are two different things.

Albert Ellis has pointed out that for years, people have blamed events in life as having automatically caused their negative emotions. Ellis has developed his A–B–C system to demonstrate the role of perceiving and thinking in emotions.

> A represents an activating event.
> C represents our consequent emotions.

Ellis has suggested that people often blame A for causing C. For example, a woman spills coffee on her new outfit. This would be an activating event, or A. She gets angry at herself for this action. She comes to believe that the event automatically caused her consequent emotion, or C.

Ellis suggests that A did not automatically cause C. The consequent emotions were caused by B, her belief or what she told herself about the event. Thus, our beliefs or our perceptions about events cause our emotions, not the events.

How can we say this? Well, we suggest that if a thousand people spilled coffee on themselves, there would be a thousand different reactions to the same event. Some of the people would be angry for hours. Some others would be angry for a few minutes and say, "Oh, well, nothing I can do about it now—I'm not going to spoil my evening because of this." Some people might even be glad it happened, because it was funny to others. Thus, you as a human being have choices in perceiving and responding to the events of your life.

Try another example to demonstrate the power of perceiver influence. Do you have a friend who seems constantly to be "down in the pits"? Listen as he or she speaks. Listen to the words and the viewpoint of life that these words reflect. Look at how this person experiences the events of his or her life. Do you ever think that regardless of what happened to this person (even positive events), he or she could turn it into a negative?

Now consider a friend who usually seems to be relatively "high" on life. Do you find that this person may turn even negative events into something more productive?

Thus, the things that happen to us in life invite us to respond in a certain manner. Courageous people are aware, however, that in the end, it's the way they look at life—not the way life is—that ultimately affects them. This is perceiver power—and you have it with you twenty-four hours a day.

Summary of Chapters 1 and 2

There are two major ways of viewing how you have become the way you are today. The first, or S→R way, suggests that you are just passively responding to stimuli. These stimuli, or influences in your life, *automatically* cause you to respond in a certain way. These influences might be parents, early childhood, teachers, relatives, friends, church, etc. Hence, the cause for your behavior is not you. The blame lies elsewhere. Blame may be on groups, other individuals, things, or even yourself. Blaming provides many secondary gains. It takes away personal responsibility, and it immobilizes you.

The more productive and courageous viewpoint is to view yourself as active and responsible for your feelings, thoughts, and actions. As opposed to the S→R model, we refer to this model as S→You→R. The "you" represents your ability to break the automatic chain of events from stimulus to response. This gives you possibilities only limited by your creativity and courage. The "you" in S→You→R is the same as Albert Ellis's concept of B or belief in his A–B–C system.

Before developing the "you" in your S→You→R, take a few moments to brush up on this chapter.

Brush Up: Chapter 2

1. Distinguish between the unproductive (Chapter 1) and the courageous way of understanding yourself.

2. Explain Assumption I: You create and determine your feelings, thoughts, and actions.

3. Discuss Assumption II: All your feelings, thoughts, and actions are pulled by your goals.

4. Discuss the difference between stated goals and unrealized goals.

5. Did you ever have a stated goal and then defeat yourself right before you reached it? If so, what might have been a fringe benefit of not reaching your stated goal?

6. What is the meaning of Assumption III: It is the way you look at life—not the way your life is—that affects you?

7. Give an example of how important your viewpoint on life is in affecting your feelings, thoughts, and actions.

8. Has your perceiving style or viewpoint on life changed in the past few years? If so, in what direction?

9. What is the difference between an S→R and an S→You→R way of understanding yourself?

10. Identify those parts of this chapter with which you disagree. Why?

11. Which parts of this chapter influenced you positively? Why?

12. What can you do differently with your life after reading Chapters 1 and 2?

ealistic ositivism: he Philosophy f Courageous People

CHAPTER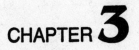

Y ou might ask why there is a chapter on philosophy included in a psychology book. To us, it is quite natural and logical to discuss philosophy in a book on self-encouragement. We have come to believe that most psychological problems are, in reality, philosophical problems. Thus, we suggest that discouraged people are not emotionally disturbed but rather philosophically disturbed. It is the errors people make in the ways they look at life that affect them and that ultimately invite their emotional and behavioral stagnation.

We believe that the starting point in developing your courage involves—not directly changing your emotions (how would you go about doing that?)—but rather correcting two basic mistakes you may make in the way you look at life.

Much discouragement is the result of two basic mistaken beliefs about self, others, and life. The first error is failing to face and accept reality as it is. The second major mistake is failing to realize all the possible alternatives still available when that reality is faced.

Discouragement occurs when people fail to overcome either of these two errors. The unwillingness of people to accept reality as it is results from a superiority complex. They place themselves out of perspective in the universe, believing that reality has "focused" in on them personally. This, of course, is naive and destructive and in its extreme, results in the feelings of grandiosity and persecution so often seen in the paranoid person.

The second basic mistake that hinders human happiness is unwillingness to realize all the possible alternatives available to people once they face and accept reality. When people make this mistake, they become overwhelmed by universal reality, giving it too much credit and blame. These people are unaware of their possibilities and feel hopeless and helpless. They are passive victims to what they see as the powerful forces of life and other people.

Either mistake, underplaying or overplaying the importance of universal reality, results in discouragement. The process of overcoming both these basic errors is perhaps the most important step to achieving a courageous life. Yet it is perhaps the most complicated task of life, as we are all victims of Error I (disrespecting reality) and Error II (disrespecting yourself).

Philosophical Error I:
Disrespecting Reality

The most frequent error people make that results in discouragement is failing to respect reality. Let's discuss some encouraging and effective ways of viewing reality.

OVERCOMING ERROR I:
RESPECTING REALITY

By facing reality, we mean either (1) accepting as fact those aspects of your life you believe cannot be changed; or (2) accepting those things and relationships you could change but in which you are unwilling to invest the time and energy necessary to do so.

People who refuse to face these realities in their lives inevitably become frustrated. Their energies become wasted in directions that are unproductive. We believe that people who fail to accept reality suffer from a superiority complex—a superiority complex, in that they believe the world was created to serve them personally and to protect them from injustices, frustrations, and unpleasantries.

How does it happen that people are invited to dodge reality and place themselves out of perspective?

ME AND FOUR BILLION OTHERS

Making Error I (disrespecting reality) reflects a loss of personal perspective in the world. There are many invitations in life to disrespect reality. For example, most people have a need to receive attention and be recognized by others. And in most well-intentioned families, certain practices occur that invite the child to lose perspective. For example, in some cultures, children come to believe that Santa Claus has personally monitored their behavior throughout the year and willingly dispenses gifts in direct proportion to their actions during that year. Think of it—isn't it a grandiose thought that in a world of over four billion people, Santa Claus will be visiting only this child at exactly midnight on the 25th of December?

This is not a criticism of this or any other family practice or custom; rather, it is an attempt to show how people become discouraged in life when they are no longer personally served. Developmental psychologists point out that children tend to go through stages where their thinking is out of perspective. The young child may believe, for example, that it gets dark out because someone has turned the light out on him because he was a bad boy. Another child may believe that thunder and lightning are punishment created for her personally, because she didn't listen to her mother. Think of it—this is clearly placing herself out of perspective—she is suffering from a superiority complex.

Most people outgrow elements of their superiority complex when they begin to realize that events in the world—traffic jams, miserable weather, diseases, etc.—are not related to them personally. Yet remnants of superiority often remain with people. Consider the following typical comments that suggest these individuals are not remembering they are sharing the globe with four billion others:

Where have you been all *my life?*
Joanne? Yes, I know her—she was in *my class.*

Can you think of other typical comments demonstrating that the speaker has lost perspective?

_____

_____

_____

If you choose to work at overcoming your superiority complex further, take a look at a globe. Look at all the countries of the world. See if you can find your city. Think about how many people four billion individuals are. If you live in a city of a hundred thousand, that means there are enough people in the world to create forty thousand cities with the same population as yours. Is it possible that things like bad weather, no parking spaces, flat tires, and so on were chosen to do you in personally?

REALITY IS NOT HERE TO DIAPER US

Alfred Adler once suggested that pampered children lose their perspective. They come to believe that they are to be served by the world as their parents served them. They become, as Albert Ellis calls them, "whiners" in the face of reality. Obviously, the anger, pouting, and other emotional manipulations that children use are no longer effective when they put themselves in perspective in the universe. Reality is just unaffected by such emotional displays. The failure of reality to comply with people's expectations then produces frustration.

The philosophy of realistic positivism suggests that it is not the job of reality to understand you—rather, it is your job to understand reality. Courageous people realize that they must go 100 percent of the way to reality—reality is not going to meet them halfway.

OVERCOMING ERROR I:
COURAGEOUS BELIEFS ABOUT REALITY

"WHAT YOU WOULD LIKE" HAS
NOTHING TO DO WITH "WHAT IS."

The favorite words of children are: "I want." Many times, these words are effective in provoking a response to the needs of the child. But soon children learn that because they want something doesn't mean they will get it. Write down a list of things that you want—and would give yourself if you were picked to run the universe:

_____

_____

_____

Now place a checkmark on those things in your list that you believe you can get and for which you are willing to make the necessary effort.

Reality has no respect for your wishes. *Reality*, again, *just is.* You have no right to demand that it be different—or for that matter—that it be the same for you as for anyone else. When you decide to accept those things that you are not willing to expend the energies to change, you are moving in the direction of overcoming Error I. And it is an effective way of achieving your goals, because that acceptance frees your energy to seek the achievable goals in your life.

Consider Zeke, who refuses to accept reality when he finds out that he has a flat tire on a cold, snowy night:

Zeke (while kicking the car): This kind of *%!?#$ thing always happens to me—I can't stand it.

Somehow, according to Zeke's logic, he personally was zeroed in on to get the flat—he is that important. And if you think that is insane, what about his idea that by kicking the car, somehow or other the flat tire will be repaired? (Is that delusion any less insane than that of the person in the mental hospital who thinks he is Napoleon?)

Now consider Sam, who has the same experience with a flat tire as Zeke:

> *Sam:* My tire is flat. I'll fix it quickly, so that I can be on my way.

Courageous people similar to Sam use their energies to move ahead in life constructively rather than getting angry at things they don't like. Courageous people are like the self-actualized people Abraham Maslow studied. Maslow (1954) wrote of these healthy human beings' ability to accept reality:

> One does not complain about water because it is wet, or about rocks because they are hard or about trees because they are green. As the child looks out upon the world with wide, uncritical innocent eyes, simply noting and observing what is the case, without either arguing the matter or demanding that it be otherwise, so does the self-actualized person look upon human nature in himself and others. [p. 207]

Courageous people start with "what is" rather than what they think "should be." A way to overcome Error I, then, is to eliminate the "shoulds," "oughts," and "musts" in your life. Each time you use one of these demands, you are losing your perspective in the world and creating a false reality. You, like Zeke, are becoming disturbed with your superiority complex.

In the place of "shoulds," "oughts," and "musts," Albert Ellis suggests some more rational ways of looking at self, other people, and the world. Ellis advises the use of "I would prefer" or "it would be better for me if" or "if I could choose, I would choose it to be this way," rather than "shoulds," "oughts," and "musts." These statements are not grandiose demands but personal preferences that are perfectly sane. Following are a few examples. Get a feel for the important difference between (1) making grandiose demands of yourself, other people, and the world and (2) expressing a personal desire.

SUPERIORITY COMPLEX: NONACCEPTANCE OF REALITY	ACCEPTANCE OF REALITY WITH A PERSONAL PREFERENCE
The Russians *shouldn't* act the way they do.	*I don't like* the way the Russians act, and *if I could choose*, I would have them act differently. But I realize that just because I would like things to be different doesn't mean that they should be different.
Prices *shouldn't* be this high. I can't stand it.	*It would be better for me* if prices weren't this high. However, ultimately I can stand it.

In summary, then, one way to accept reality is to realize that *reality is the way it is and is independent of what you want it to be or think it should be.* Another way to overcome Error I is to accept another element of reality—it is not fair!

REALITY IS NOT FAIR—
SO DON'T DEMAND AND EXPECT IT TO BE SO

Julia: It just isn't fair—Carolyn can eat all the pastry, cakes, and cookies that she wants, and she never gains a pound. And yet if I just look at food, I put on weight.

We ask you: "To whom does Julia take her complaint?" Julia is producing her own frustration because she believes it is not fair that the universe is more kind to Carolyn than it is to her. Her frustration is not due to the fact that she gains weight but is related to her unwillingness to accept reality the way it is.

We ask Julia: "Who said things are fair? Why must it be fair? Prove that it must be fair." Obviously it cannot be proven. Thus, Julia is destining herself to a life of frustration, because she does not accept an element of the world that does not work in her favor.

We might mention to Julia: "It doesn't seem fair that you have two cars, a healthy heart, three meals a day, and no major diseases—and even that you are alive today when so many people are starving, ill, or not even living by your age."

Justice seekers—like Julia—are often selective in deciding what is just. They want justice but on their grounds. This, of course, is why the world has conflicts. Listen to labor–management negotiations when each side describes what is fair. Often they are miles apart in their interpretations of justice. Or listen to parent–child discussions as both parties describe what is fair.

It is important for us to say here that justice is a most noteworthy ideal and that we are leading the parade for a more just world. Courageous people even actively choose to achieve the goals of justice. In the process of accepting reality and overcoming Error I, courageous people assess whether (1) justice in a certain circumstance can be achieved and (2) whether or not they are willing to use the necessary time and energy to achieve it. They realize that immobilized whining and barroom demanding of justice are not only ineffective but frustrating.

The philosophy of realistic positivism suggests that people start with what is—not what should be or what they would like or even what is fair. They seek a clear understanding of the rules that the universe has set forth as the starting point to move toward their goals. This is the realistic element in realistic positivism. Once people accept the "what is" of reality, a whole new world of possibilities opens up to them—if they don't make Error II.

Philosophical Error II:
Disrespecting Yourself

The rules reality sets forth are determined by reality, not by you. These rules continue to exist regardless of your personal feelings toward them. "You do not control the universe," Albert Ellis says. However, the good news is that you have full control over your own personal interpretation of reality. And it is this—your own personal viewpoint on the world—that ultimately affects you, as was suggested in Assumption III (Chapter 2).

You, as a human being, have a remarkable capacity for perceptual and behavioral change. Lazarus and Fay (1975) wrote: "Humans, unlike any other animals, have an almost instant capacity for change" (p. 16).

Change in people's lives can be on many levels. People can change the way they look at life (perceptual change) or the way they act in life (behavioral change). We believe that courageous people take personal responsibility for making those changes that will lead to more effective long-range goal attainment. This is the positive component of the philosophy of realistic positivism. Overcoming Error II, then, is realizing that you have limitless possibilities in life once you accept certain inflexible rules of reality.

OVERCOMING ERROR II
THROUGH PERCEPTUAL ALTERNATIVES

We believe that the more ways you have of looking at life, the more capable you are of living fully and adjusting to life. Discouraged people have a tendency to view life in a rigid, stereotypical, black-and-white fashion. They tend to react the same way to situations without generating creative and workable perceptions. Everything seems to be clear-cut to discouraged people. This keeps them restricted and limits their choices and experiences.

You can develop your skills in coping with life to reach your goals by developing your perceptual alternatives. In *Turning People On* (Losoncy, 1977), we introduced the concept of perceptual alternatives. It refers to the many different ways of viewing and interpreting any given situation.

You are a bundle of complex and creative talents. In any given situation, you possess the ability to size up a situation and perceive it in many ways if you choose. From the many perceptions you generate, you can choose the most effective, realistic perception. Consider a few exercises borrowed from *Turning People On* (Losoncy, 1977) to develop your perceptual alternatives.

EXERCISE 1

Think about a situation in which you felt bad. It might have been failing a test or a "put-down" by someone. For example, if it was failing a test, you could view that test failure in many different ways. Some ways might include:

1. I must study much harder for the next test.

2. School isn't for me. I studied as hard as I could and I didn't make it.

3. That stupid teacher has something against me.

4. I didn't put the right answers in the correct places.

5. I knew I'd fail. Mom and Dad were right when they told me I was taking courses that were too ambitious.

6. I'll learn from this. Mistakes are nothing more than suggestions that there are alternative answers or better responses. [p. 66]

Some or all of these ways of viewing test failure may be facts. Think for a moment about each of the six ways of viewing that same reality, the test failure. How do you feel if you choose the third way of viewing the failure? How about the sixth way? Notice the different reactions you have to the same external reality? That is the perceiving power present in all human beings!

For you, which is the most productive way of viewing this failure? By "productive," we mean the way that involves facing reality and that will generate courageous movement on your part. Now try Exercise 2.

EXERCISE 2

Someone teases you about a physical characteristic of yours about which you are extremely sensitive. Generate as many ways as you can to perceive their teasing:

_____

_____

_____

Which perceptual alternative is the most productive? Remember, productive means that it includes facing reality and that it generates courage and movement on your part. Now try this with an object (pencil, paper clip, etc.) currently available to you:

EXERCISE 3

Stand above the object and study it. Now look at it from the sides and concentrate. Pick it up, if possible. Consider the different ways of viewing that object. How is the object different according to the different ways you look at it? Do this for one minute, allowing your mind unlimited freedom. Jot down your responses:

_____

_____

_____

Imagine! If you could find this many ways of viewing this one object in one minute, think about how many ways you have of viewing yourself, your complexity, and any circumstances or events in your life!

If you feel a sense of power over yourself—you are developing perceptual alternatives, and even more importantly, you are on the road to greater self-encouragement. And again we ask you: "Is there a greater gift that you can give yourself?"

There have been many inspiring human experiences demonstrating the importance of having this ability of perceptual alternatives.

Viktor Frankl in *Man's Search for Meaning* (1959) wrote about his experience of being imprisoned in a war camp with little chance for survival. He described how the guards stripped him, starved him, dehumanized him. He said that the prison guards could treat him any way they chose (external reality), but the one thing they couldn't do was to affect the way he chose to view his existence (perceptual alternatives).

Epictetus, the Stoic philosopher, wrote: "Disease is an impediment to the body [external reality], but not to the mind unless the will chooses it [perceptual alternatives]."

William Glasser, the founder of Reality Therapy, discussed alternatives in *Current Psychotherapies* (Glasser & Zunin, 1973) when he wrote:

> Even a man facing a firing squad has *some* limited alternatives. He might pray, curse, collapse, spit, hold his breath, scream, try to escape to the best of his ability, face the firing squad with equanimity, bite his lip, stick out his tongue, and so on. [p. 297]

Rollo May, the noted psychoanalyst, commented on an interview with a patient on death row. Discussing his time in prison, the patient said, "A man can live without liberty [his prison experience—external reality], but he cannot live without freedom of will [perceptual alternatives]."

Alfred Adler saw this sense of perceptual alternatives and self-determination when he wrote: "Do not forget the most important fact that neither heredity nor environment are determining factors. Both are giving only the frame and the influence [external reality] which are answered by the individual in regard to his styled creative power [perceptual alternatives]" (p. xxiv).

These writings are examples of how perceptual alternatives can improve the quality of your one life on the globe. If some of these individuals facing extreme stress could generate courage through, first, facing their real situation and, second, developing the most productive way of viewing their situation, imagine what you can do in your everyday life! Must you be confronted with your own death to appreciate the beauty of your life?

We believe that once you have developed your perceptual alternatives to view life's events, you are then in a better position to deal with these events. We suggest that perceptual alternatives show the potential path to behavior change. Responsible human beings choose the best behavioral alternative from among their many perceptual alternatives. Behavioral change is elaborated upon in Chapter 7 and is, of course, the goal of self-encouragement.

Brush Up: Chapter 3

1. Describe Error I. Give a few examples of making Error I.

2. Why does the person who makes Error I suffer from a superiority complex?

3. Why is it so common for people to make Error I?

4. Describe Error II. Give a few examples of making Error II.

5. What are perceptual alternatives? How can developing perceptual alternatives help a person to cope?

6. Can you see a relationship between perceptual alternatives and the S→You→R model from Chapter 2? If so, detail the relationship.

7. Why would a self-help psychology book include a chapter on philosophy?

8. With what points in the chapter would you disagree?

9. Are there points in the chapter that hit home?

10. What parts of the chapter can you use in the future?

11. How does this chapter relate to Chapter 1: "An Unproductive Way of Understanding Yourself," and to Chapter 2: "A Courageous Way of Understanding Yourself"?

Building a Positive Relationship with Yourself

CHAPTER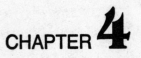

N o doubt you have spent countless hours struggling with the important question, "Who am I?" Perhaps, from time to time, you have even found what you believed to be the answer. This is especially true if you have ever said, "This is the kind of person I am."

EXAMPLE 1
Joanne (age 17): Are you going to the class party?

Marilyn: No, I went last time, and everybody was such a snob and ignored me. And I'm the kind of person *who will give people one chance to accept me, and that's it.*

EXAMPLE 2
John: Who, me, pass math?! You must be kidding—*I have no math ability at all.*

EXAMPLE 3
Wanda: I'm *too shy* to meet boys. I'm the kind of person who is worried about what people think of me.

EXAMPLE 4
Leon: I *can't resist snacks* around the house.

Marilyn, John, Wanda, and Leon have found what they believe to be themselves. Marilyn's identity is one who gives other people one chance before closing the door to them. John is the kind of person who has no math ability. Wanda is the kind of person who is shy. Leon is the kind of person who lacks will power in resisting tempting snacks. Include some "I'm the kind of person" beliefs about yourself:

_____

_____

_____

We think that these self-beliefs are often comfortable, yet these identities may be self-defeating. After all, knowing what you believe to be facts about yourself gives you clues about how you might behave in various situations. For example, if you are convinced that you have a shy identity, you can continue acting shyly, thus never facing the possibility of rejection. In this way, however, you will never experience a good active personal relationship. Or you might be the kind of person, like Leon, who can't resist snacks, despite the fact that you might want to lose weight. This identity gives you an excuse to continue your eating behavior. You might conclude, "How do you expect a person who cannot resist snacks to act when faced with snacks?" Naturally, he or she eats them.

We believe it is absurd, incorrect, and even self-defeating to draw conclusions about yourself. Some psychologists, for example, have pointed out the damage that sometimes results from drawing conclusions or labeling someone. A psychologist might conclude that a patient is paranoid. This "diseased" identity then gives the person permission to act paranoid. Such identities, then, provide the blueprints for patients to draw from when choosing how to act.

Believing that you are a certain type of person implies that somewhere or other, there is a real you. We ask, "How do you know the real you?" You may suggest that you have observed your actions and feelings in the past. For example, you may have noticed over a period of time that when confronted with tests in school, you immediately panic and forget everything. So you naturally have come to believe that *you are the kind of person who panics when taking tests*.

We believe that it is absurd, inaccurate, and even self-defeating to draw conclusions about yourself. You are such a complex bundle of possibilities that your identity can never be solidified while you have life.

We will not argue with your observation that in the past, you panicked when facing a test. We trust that your observations are accurate. However, we will ask for a little openness from you to challenge the conclusions you draw from those observations. Consider a few questions:

1. What possible fringe benefits do you receive from teachers and friends by saying, "I'm the kind of person who panics at a test, and then I don't do well"?

Teachers: _____

Friends: _____

2. Did you panic at *every* test you took in your life? Can you think of one test where you didn't panic?

_____

_____

_____

3. If you walk into a test totally believing that you are *the kind of person who panics at a test*—what is the most likely way you will react?

_____

_____

_____

4. Except for the fringe benefits you receive, as you have discussed above, how do you think that panicking at a test will help your score? Perhaps you believe that you panic for fear of doing poorly. But we ask you, "Will the panic help your score?" What do you believe the results of test panic are for you?

_____

_____

_____

5. Consider: What if every time in your life you panicked in a test situation? Does that mean you will panic every time in the future?

One of your errors in logic is that from noticing a pattern in your past (panicking in a test situation), you have jumped to treating merely an observation (which was accurate) as a fact (which wasn't proven). Consider the following analogy. Some Martians have come to Earth to gather some data about the average size of an Earthling. Imagine that these Martians happen to land near Mt. Rushmore and see the huge faces of the four former American presidents carved in granite. If they stayed no longer to get a better sample, they would be greatly misled. They would have treated an observation (which was accurate) as though it were a fact (which was certainly inaccurate).

> Get off your past—right now you are your present, and
> you will never be your past.

The first way of turning on your courage is to realize that *now you are your present and not your past*. We suggest that you get off your past. We suspect that there was a time in your past when you said "I can't tie my shoes" or "I can't drive a car," but now you can. What if you had never tried to overcome your can't and had concluded that this was the kind of person you were? If so, even today you would not be able to tie your shoes or drive a car. Somewhere, at some point, you altered your identity and energized your courage. It is only after you work hard at changing your rigid identity that you can move on to unlimited accomplishments. Can you think of previous rigid identities or self-defeating beliefs you once had that you worked hard to overcome?

PAST IDENTITY   NEW IDENTITY

I can't . . .   _____

I'm the kind of person
who . . .   _____

_____   _____

_____   _____

Congratulations! Take a moment to feel that sense of accomplishment over your own worst enemy—you and your self-defeating identity.

A Flowing Identity

We believe that as people become courageous and responsible, they move in the direction this chart indicates from left to right:

DISCOURAGING IDENTITY	→ COURAGEOUS IDENTITY
Rigid, fixed, unchangeable	→ Constantly changing
Identity carved in granite	→ Identity like an exciting, flowing river
Planner	→ Spontaneous
Procrastinator	→ Doer
Passive	→ Active

Finally: *If your identity of the past was based on your actions of the past, your present moment will be part of your past in the future. So you can change your future by changing your self-defeating identities of the present.*

Make a commitment to change some rigid identity of yourself. List those past *observations* that you have made about yourself. In a courageous manner, put these observations in their place. Where would you like to go?

OBSERVATIONS————————→
From (This is the way I was)	*To* (This is the way I'll be)
_____	_____
_____	_____
_____	_____

Stop for a moment! Feel the sense of potential newness. You have started to reenergize your courage. Think of the exciting possibilities if you follow through on your commitment. It's up to you. We believe that your new, flowing identity can best be garnished with some other elements, like respect and trust in yourself.

RESPECT AND TRUST IN YOURSELF

Abraham Maslow (1954), whom we mentioned in Chapter 3, was one of the few psychologists who was interested in studying the healthy person. He observed and assessed thousands of people to determine those ingredients present in the most capable human beings. He wanted to find out if there were characteristic patterns present in those people he came to call self-actualized. Two of the key characteristics Maslow found in self-actualized people were respect for and trust in themselves.

Have you ever had these feelings of trust and respect for yourself—feelings that you believed in yourself and recognized that you were the most important judge of your actions, even though other people felt differently. Give an example:

_____

_____

_____

Feel that sense of mastery as you relive the occasion!

Self-actualized people trust their personal evaluations about their lives above the opinions of others. This does not mean that they are closed to the attitudes of other people. Rather, they are quite open to new ideas. Self-actualized people view new ideas as a potential source of personal growth. They spend their energies growing in new directions rather than defending where they are. They have less of a need to conform, to agree, or to seek approval for acceptance sake. Self-actualized people tend to judge each issue on the facts, not on what they want the facts to be or what others think the facts are. Their source of evaluation and sense of personal security come from within rather than being external.

Carl Rogers (1961) noted that clients in psychotherapy tend to move in this direction—from external to internal trust:

> The individual increasingly comes to feel that this locus of evaluation lies within himself. Less and less does he look to others for approval or disapproval; for standards to live by; for decisions and choices. He recognizes that it rests within himself to choose; that the only question which matters is, "Am I living in a way which is deeply satisfying to me, and which truly expresses me?" [p. 119]

Of course, trusting yourself is a courageous decision. When you do so, you are responsible. Remember how easy life was when you were a child and all your needs and responsibilities were taken care of by others? Growing up involves taking on increasing levels of personal responsibility. Some people choose to retreat from the demands of life and continue to force others to assume their responsibilities. These "externals" are talented in using their weakness to manipulate others into rescuing them from the responsibilities of life. Rarely do they get the chance to feel that sense of personal accomplishment.

> Todd, 13, cried to his parents whenever he was faced with collecting his money from the customers on his paper route. In this weekly ritual, inevitably, his well-meaning parents would decide to pitch in and help.

Todd was learning to rely on others for his personal responsibility. His well-intentioned parents felt that they were only helping him. However, when they assisted him, they were demonstrating to Todd that he was incapable. Todd was developing the life-style and the identity of a person who couldn't handle responsibility by himself. Can you remember times when you used inadequacy and irresponsibility like Todd?

_____

_____

_____

Remember in Chapter 2 when we described the importance of looking at behavior as being governed by goals or results? Was your behavior effective in inviting other people to take over your responsibilities?

Self-respect is hindered not only by the desire to get other people to take over personal responsibilities but also by a lack of self-confidence. The more uncertain people are about themselves, the more they need approval and directions from external sources. If people are to help themselves, they need to realize that their decisions are theirs and not the responsibility of anyone else. What fringe benefits do people receive when they shift their responsibilities to others?

_____

_____

_____

So, people with self-respect and self-trust believe that they are responsible for their decisions and their lives. They also have a confidence that they can make the best effort possible to overcome their problems and achieve their goals in life.

With true self-respect and self-trust, you face it all and stand tall. You welcome and even enjoy taking full responsibility for your life. You are the rare minority when you accept responsibility. You constantly let yourself know that you and only you are responsible.

This, of course, includes the responsibility for opening yourself to all possible information from available sources for making the best decisions. But in the end, the responsibility for the final decision is yours. You trust your judgments, your opinions, and your evaluations. Though you certainly enjoy when other people agree with your beliefs and even like you as a person—that is up to them. In the end, you are ultimately accountable to only one person—you.

With true self-respect, you face it all and stand tall. You welcome and even enjoy taking full responsibility for your life. When you accept full responsibility for your life, you become one of a rare and courageous minority.

FROM DISRESPECT FOR SELF	TO SELF-RESPECT
My environment or other people are responsible.	I am responsible.
Someone else said so—so it must be. Everybody does it—so I should.	Even though someone else said so, it does not make sense to me—and I am responsible for me.
	Even though everybody else does it, it doesn't make sense to me—and I am responsible for me.

Each time you take on additional responsibility, feel that personal pride. Feel that growing strength. Feel that willingness to accept and be responsible for your decisions—right or wrong and wherever they may lead. You chose and the choice is yours and no one else's. Each day, take more and more control of your life.

PERSONAL COURAGE EXERCISE 1

Make a plan each day to develop increasing trust in yourself and your decisions. Think of people to whom you have turned for answers, and increasingly find those answers within yourself. How can you move toward self-respect and self-trust?

_____

_____

_____

PERSONAL COURAGE EXERCISE 2

Think of some of the things you have been told about yourself, other people, or life that did not quite make sense to you. Today, challenge these ideas, and ask yourself, "Do I have to be continually talked into things that I don't believe?" Itemize some ideas.

_____

_____

_____

PERSONAL COURAGE EXERCISE 3

What can you do to demonstrate to yourself that you are in the process of overcoming these ideas? Develop a plan.

_____

_____

_____

Focusing on Your Resources

LIABILITY FOCUSING

Julie (age 45): I'd like to go to college, but it's been almost thirty years since I was in high school. I think it would be too hard.

Julie: Yes, but a big part of college success depends on a person's ability to write and I'm not that good of a writer.

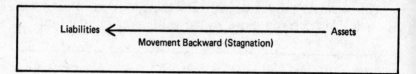

ASSET FOCUSING
Julie: Yes, but I have been reading regularly and keeping up with what is going on in the world.

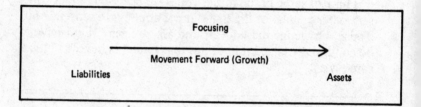

Have you ever engaged in this sort of asset–liability volleyball with yourself? Discouragement involves focusing on your weaknesses, your liabilities, which invites you to lower your self-esteem and feelings of worth. Julie demonstrates the lack of a flowing identity when she says, "I'm not that good of a writer." Here she implies that perhaps she was marked "poor writer" and that it was carved in granite. Again, be aware of the fringe benefits of this rigid identity. What are some benefits of Julie's choice of focusing on her liabilities?

_____

_____

_____

The arrows demonstrate the movement that takes place in her monologue. When Julie focuses on and stresses her negative points, she discourages herself. But she does go on to show herself a resource that might be of assistance to her success in college. In these courageous moments, she is doing positive focusing, and thus the arrows demonstrate potential positive movement.

Construct a dialogue with yourself, demonstrating asset and liability focusing. Talk to yourself about a goal you would like to achieve but where you fear potential failure. Write down some things you could tell yourself that could move you toward and away from your goal. Construct arrows that demonstrate whether each sentence is an asset or a liability focusing.

LIABILITY FOCUSING   ASSET FOCUSING
(STAGNATION)   (MOVEMENT)

←————————————   ————————————→

——————————————   ——————————————

——————————————   ——————————————

——————————————   ——————————————

Self-talk is vital to self-encouragement (Zastrow, 1979). Did you find that you were able to establish more control of yourself with your self-talk? Self-encouragement is the process of focusing on your resources in order to build your self-esteem and self-confidence. By constructively focusing on your resources and potential, you enhance the chance of moving toward your stated goals.

As a human being, you are an exciting, complex person with a mind that has so much potential; it is unfathomable. Just imagine: At any given moment, you have the capability of thinking about any experience of your whole life, positively or negatively interpreted by you. You can remember your moments of failure, embarrassment, or the times when you mastered something you hoped to do for a long time.

We encourage you to reflect on your complexity. Think about all the different dimensions in which you could consider yourself. For example, you might think about yourself in your ability to read, write, spell, dance, or cook. This can be expanded to include such specifics as your ability to read history books or magazines. There are no limits except those of your awareness. Take only a minute to jot in all the different dimensions on which you could think about yourself (please use more paper if you need it):

1. _____   7. _____

2. _____   8. _____

3. _____   9. _____

4. _____   10. _____

5. _____   11. _____

6. _____   12. _____

Now do an *asset analysis* on yourself. Here are some areas to consider as a starting point:

Physical resources _____

Mental/intellectual resources _____

Emotional resources _____

Social resources _____

Spiritual resources _____

Personality resources _____

But by all means don't limit yourself only to these areas.

When you consider yourself in this light, you can do a potentiality analysis. A potentiality analysis involves thinking about all the things you are capable of being as a result of your available and untapped resources.

You + Courage = Anything

Take a few minutes to do a potentiality analysis. What are your hidden resources? What liabilities do you currently have that can be turned into resources (e.g., stubbornness to steadfastness)?

_____

_____

_____

Keep working at understanding and appreciating your potential resources. They are always available within you—but the responsibility for bringing your resources into the foreground is yours.

We have discussed the importance, in building a relationship with oneself, of having flowing identity, self-respect, and an understanding of and focus on your resources. Now we discuss putting it all together with the enthusiasm you have to become a fuller self. Enthusiasm helps you bring out what Carl Rogers calls your personal power.

> Your resources are always within you. It is your responsibility to bring these strengths into your awareness to assist you in attaining your goals.

Enthusiasm

Have you ever observed people at a restaurant having an early breakfast? Some people come in yawning, rubbing their eyes, and talking about the oncoming day as though it were specially designed to destroy them. At the same restaurant, there are other people who show a high energy level in which they enthusiastically ponder the possibilities they will make out of this new day. Their life is seen as having opportunities and potential accomplishments. They are alive and moving toward their goals. At this early morning hour, people are at the "starting gates" for their day.

Think of how much potential you have during any one hour or day. In any one day, you could travel from New York to Chicago to Los Angeles to Hawaii, having a meal in each city. In any one day, you could see the Eiffel Tower in France, the pyramids in Egypt, and the kangaroos of Australia. In one day, as well, a whole community could be wiped out.

Consider what happened in Guyana and Nagasaki. It is also possible for a person to sleep twenty-four hours in one day or watch twenty hours of TV.

We believe that your flowing identity, self-respect, and awareness of your resources are vital to the development of your courage. But whether or not you eventually actualize your courage is related to your level of enthusiasm and energy. You can function like the hopeless yawner at breakfast, overwhelmed by the anticipation of the demands of the day. Or you can be more like the person who is excited to be alive, to have choices, and to make a real contribution to self, other people, and the world, beginning at this valuable moment.

Jot down some things you could tell youself, or that you have heard energyless people tell themselves, to justify immobility or inaction. For example, "What's the use?" "My boss will shoot down the idea anyway." "I didn't get enough sleep."

_____

_____

_____

What are the fringe benefits of adopting this nonenthusiastic way of looking at life?

_____

_____

_____

Yes, it is quite easy to smoke an extra cigarette, drink an extra cup of coffee, and blame and complain about the misery of life rather than energetically facing and changing it.

William James, one of the early American psychologists, suffered severe depression and was suicidal at frequent periods of his life. He pondered the uselessness of his life and saw no sense in going on. He believed that nothing really mattered. It seemed to serve no purpose to try harder if everything meant nothing anyway.

James wrote a friend of his and expressed his hopeless view of life. James's friend wrote back to him and suggested that he believe in himself and see the importance of his own accomplishments and contributions. It was up to him (nothing outside of him) to develop meaning, purpose, and energy to fulfill himself. His friend concluded, believe in yourself for just one day, just to see how it works.

James took his friend's advice. He realized that it was up to him to create his purposes and goals. He recognized that by talking himself into believing that his life was meaningless, he was excusing his immobilization. In later years, James went on to make a major contribution to the development of the philosophy of pragmatism. Not coincidentally, pragmatism is a philosophy that suggests that "whatever works, is truth." For James, it was more effective to adopt a positive, energetic way of life. When his attitude changed, so did his enthusiasm for life. Students of psychology and philosophy today continue to read and be inspired by the writings of James. No doubt, he will continue to be read for many years.

Your own enthusiasm, like the created enthusiasm of James, springs from your philosophy or viewpoint of life as well as from the goals that you yourself establish. It is your own responsibility to energize yourself. Recognize your role in developing a productive viewpoint on life as well as goals that give you the pulling power.

If you are still skeptical, we again beg your openness to a few questions:

1. Who, if not you, is responsible for developing your goals? What are the fringe benefits of believing that your purpose in life must come from outside of you?

_____

_____

_____

2. If you believe that you are not an enthusiastic person, how do you think this lack of energy happened? Some people see themselves as unenthusiastic. We ask, "When sperm and egg unite at conception, are some stamped with 'This will be an enthusiastic person,' whereas others are stamped with, 'This will not be an enthusiastic person'?" Some people argue that their metabolism is too low. We are somewhat inclined to

believe that the biological explanation has some support. However, we also believe that your metabolism, your diet, etc., may only provide some limitations to your energy. Consequently, some people have a more difficult time developing enthusiasm due to biological and physiological factors. However, it is the responsibility of each person to function at the higher limits of his or her abilities.

Consider Gretchen, age 8, who sits wearily on her front step, elbows on her knees and hands supporting her unhappy face. She is the picture of boredom. She ponders over the waste of a day off from school with nothing to do. Passersby note the lack of energy this girl appears to have. Then Lisa, Gretchen's neighbor, comes out of her house shouting, "Want to jump rope with me, Gretchen?" Gretchen's eyes brighten, a wide smile appears, and she zooms across the lawn with unlimited energies.

Gretchen's goals have pulling power. What appeared to be physical fatigue was really just the lack of a purpose that generates enthusiasm.

3. Can you remember times when you, like Gretchen, felt tired or sleepy until something happened that gave you energy?

_____

_____

_____

4. Have you ever found yourself in a slump, where you lay around the house sleeping many, many hours and still felt sleepy? Did you get any fringe benefits from this?

_____

_____

_____

We believe that there are many ways of developing your enthusiasm. At the base of any energetic philosophy of life is personal responsibility for developing a constructive view of life and one's goals. We suggest a positive movement from left to right on your part:

DISCOURAGING OUTLOOK →	ENCOURAGING, ENTHUSIASTIC VIEWPOINT
Someone else is responsible for my purpose and goals in life.	I am responsible for my purpose and goals in life.
I'll associate with blamers and negative complainers.	I'll choose to associate with energetic people who have a positive outlook.
I'll listen to music and read books that reflect hopelessness.	I'll listen to music and read books that reflect positive values.
I'll go about tomorrow, aimlessly hoping that meaning will arrive with the morning newspaper.	I'll plan goals today for tomorrow; I have a reason to wake up tomorrow.
Tomorrow is just another day.	Tomorrow is special.
Look at how miserable this weather is.	Isn't it great that I am alive to see this weather—however miserable it might appear to be.

Look at yourself and your life! You are alive—this is your moment in the history of the universe. You have possibilities because you are alive. But time moves on. Get out of the quicksand of negativism, and, like James, make the most of the moment. It will never return.

Brush Up: Chapter 4

1. Why is it suggested that having a rigid identity may be detrimental to the development of your courage? Do you agree?

2. What is the meaning of a flowing identity?

3. Is your identity an observation or a fact? Support your position.

4. What was one of the key patterns Maslow found in the healthy, self-actualized persons he studied?

5. What is the meaning of internal rather than external points of personal evaluation?

6. What is asset focusing? Do asset focusing with yourself for a few minutes. How do you feel when you take the time to asset focus?

7. Did you have teachers who did liability focusing on you? How did you feel around these teachers?

8. Review your potentiality analysis. Now that some time has passed since you made the analysis, can you add some items to it?

9. Take a few minutes, and consider how many things—if you worked to your fullest—you could accomplish in the next twenty-four hours. Write them in below.

_____

_____

_____

10. Just imagine how many things you could do in your lifetime! Consider some long-range goals.

11. What songs, books, movies, or friends can you identify that give you energy and enthusiasm or that just plain "turn you on"?

Speaking in Courageous Language

 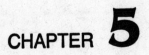

The way people look at life is what ultimately affects their behavior. And words play a role in creating images that affect how people see events in life. People who are depressed, for example, speak with a self-effacing vocabulary that further deepens their low. Courageous people, on the contrary, speak in optimistic, rational language. The importance of words is seen everywhere.

Salespeople, for example, are quite aware of how important it is to use the right word at the right time to influence buying behavior. Consider how the use of words can alter emotional reactions. Look at two ways of describing the same meal on a dinner menu:

> Open-faced, hickory-smoked steak garnished with mushrooms in a Bordelaise sauce complemented by Idaho's finest potatoes.
>
> Chopped steak sandwich with French fries.

Interestingly, the seductive vocabulary used in the first example might attract two times the cost of the second!

By the same token, your vocabulary affects your courage. The words you use in everyday life have a powerful influence on your feelings, thoughts, and actions. We are certainly not concluding that your lanugage creates your emotions and beliefs. We do believe, however, that language, emotions, beliefs, and behaviors all influence each other simultaneously, as you function as a whole, complete person. Thus, by altering your language to make it more rational, you can alter your feelings, beliefs, and behavior to develop your courage.

The subtle or not so subtle words that you choose to use affect your level of courage. Consider this shop steward who wanted to influence his constituents' voting behavior:

> Management is treading on you and rubbing your faces in the dirt. They are laughing at you and are calling you "stupid" as they drive their big cars out of here.

Obviously, management wasn't literally rubbing the workers' faces in the dirt. But this shop steward realized the emotional effectiveness of words. The selection of certain words can enhance anger, depression, or any other emotion. In this example, the steward was inviting further anger to influence voting behavior.

Think of how you feel when you are depressed. What words might you use to convince yourself of your hopelessness and helplessness? Jot in a few comments you might tell yourself to accelerate your depression:

_____

_____

_____

Yes, these words may further enhance your depression. But, what are the fringe benefits of this type of language?

_____

_____

_____

At any given moment you can choose to use courageous or unproductive language. Courageous language is rational and responsible. We next suggest some ways to make your language more courageous.

Be Active and Responsible

The helpless person speaks passively. Passive language, as discussed in Chapter 1, suggests that the individual is just helplessly responding to the all-powerful, controlling external forces. The helpless person is suggesting, "It was not my responsibility that I acted this way—rather, something else was the cause for my misdeed—and any other reasonable person would have had to act in exactly the same way as I did given this same set of circumstances." Although we agree that in many instances, perhaps many people would act in a similar way, we have no doubt that there are very few situations in which everyone would act exactly the same way.

Consider what Troy believes to be a helpless action:

Troy: I punched my boss in the mouth.

Ed: Why?

Troy: He was hassling me.

Ed: Did you talk to him first?

Troy: No, I just couldn't stand the hassling anymore, and I lost control.

Troy blamed the boss for his (Troy's) punch. Granted, Troy may have been in a difficult situation, feeling hassled all the time. Yet the punch was the decision and action of Troy. The passive language suggests that the punch was an automatic response to the hassle. Saying "I lost control" is another form of passive language. "I lost control" provides an excellent way for Troy to justify not taking full responsibility for his behavior. We suggest that Troy *chose* to punch his boss and that Troy *chose* to lose control. Remember Assumptions II and III in Chapter 2? This is an example of the unrealized goal winning in the struggle. How would Troy express himself more actively than in the previous dialogue?

> *Troy:* I decided to punch my boss in his mouth.
>
> *Ed.:* Why?
>
> *Troy:* I made myself angry by telling myself that he was hassling me. So I thought that this was the most productive action on my part.
>
> *Ed:* Did you talk to him?
>
> *Troy:* No. I decided that talking to him would be unproductive, and so my decision was to lose control.

It is important to emphasize that we are not trying to tell Troy whether he should choose to punch or not to punch people when he feels hassled. All we are suggesting is that if Troy is to take fuller charge of his life, he can begin by speaking more responsibly.

PASSIVE, HELPLESS LANGUAGE	ACTIVE, COURAGEOUS LANGUAGE
You made me act this way	I *chose* to act this way because of how I responded to you.
I lost control when . . .	I *chose* to lose control when . . .
I had to . . .	I *decided* . . .
This weather makes me . . .	I *make myself* . . . when we get weather like this.
My stomach pains kept me home.	I *decided* to stay home when I had stomach pains.

Active, courageous people use words like *choose, decided, made, forced myself.*

Get Off Your Can't

Two other passive forms of language are *can't* and *if only*.

> A human *can't* be fertilized out of the womb.
> A four-minute mile *can't* possibly be done by a person.
> The United States *can't* possibly establish relations with China.
> Never will an object be created that can fly.

Complete these sentences with the first thoughts that you develop:

I can't   _____

I can't   _____

I can't   _____

I can't   _____

Examine your "can'ts"! In any of these examples, could you substitute the word *won't* for *can't*? When you use "can't," you imply that "never, under any conditions whatsoever, could I achieve this." In some instances, "I won't" is a more responsible way of expressing your lack of action. Look at the Courage Direction Chart in Chapter 2. How does saying "I won't" differ from saying "I can't"?

CAN'T	WON'T
_____	_____
_____	_____
_____	_____

"Won't" implies that "I'm not willing to invest the time, energy, money, or risk to make this change." Saying "can't" implies that "even if I did, nothing could possibly happen."

We believe that some "can'ts" do exist. For example, "I can't keep from dying at some point" is probably fairly accurate as far as the evidence that has accumulated so far about life span is concerned. Some people even question this idea as a "can't." You, of course, must decide for yourself as to the validity of the no-die "can't." We encourage you to become sensitive to your use of the word *can't*. What are the fringe benefits of using the word *can't*?

_____

_____

_____

It's so unusual for people to take responsibility for their lives that it shocks others when they do. People aren't accustomed to this sort of responsibility taking. Can you imagine:

I won't make it to work today—I'm sick.

So, we believe that there are responsible and irresponsible "can'ts." An irresponsible "can't" is really a "won't" that lacks courage.

I can't tell my mother that I'm sick and tired of her abuse.
I can't memorize poems.

We suggest that in both instances, a "won't" could probably be substituted for the "can't." In the first example, the individual needs more courage, and in the second instance, perhaps a little or a lot more effort is needed.

Responsible "can'ts" are high-probability facts:

> I can't fly by myself.
> I can't live in the year 1800 anymore.

Be sensitive to your use of the word *can't*. By changing irresponsible "can'ts" to "won'ts," you can take charge of an aspect of your life that you previously may not have addressed. You are now steps ahead of where you were.

It is inappropriate for you to feel guilty for the vast number of times you realize that your "can't" is really a "won't." Guilt tends to be unproductive and immobilizing. It is important, however, just to realize that "I could, but I choose not to—and that's OK." The biggest "won't," then, is to say "I won't feel guilty about using 'won't' instead of 'can't.'"

Eliminate "If Only . . . , Then I. . . ." Sentences

Another passive phrase is the one that begins wtih "If only. . . . " Complete this sentence:

> If only it weren't for _____, then my life would be great.

Were you able to find an "if only" in your life? "If only" phrases neatly explain your behavior through outside factors. Using these phrases gives you the luxury of making yourself a passive responder to events outside yourself. Consider some "if only" statements:

> If only I didn't have this headache, everything would be so great.

If only my parents weren't fighting last night, I could have studied and done better on that test.

If only I wasn't born in this environment, I could have been successful.

What are the fringe benefits of these "if only" statements? Consider this "if only" dialogue described by the late psychiatrist Eric Berne:

Husband: *If only* my wife wouldn't nag, I wouldn't drink.

Wife: *If only* my husband wouldn't drink, I wouldn't nag.

They are in an "if only" cycle. Each of their "if onlys" is the cause of their behavior—and each person's behavior is the other person's "if only."

These "if only" cycles are quite common in relationships. Notice again that both husband and wife are acting as helpless responders. Neither person is willing to take responsibility to stop the destructive cycle. In reality, the husband drinks because he chooses to drink, and the wife nags because she chooses to nag. It is only when each individual realizes that "I, not you, am responsible for my behavior," that each person can take charge of his or her life.

"If onlys" are destructive to reaching your goals. "If onlys" often stop you at crucial times in your movement forward. You, as a human being, are quite talented in justifying your forward push through those "if onlys." "If onlys" are governed by your unrealized goals.

We are sensitive to the belief that it may be more difficult for some people to reach their goals than for others due to external factors. For example, a person who was not born in an environment of financial abundance may find it more difficult than someone with this advantage to own a fancy car or a beautiful home. It also may be more difficult for the short person to become a professional basketball player than it would be for someone else who is taller. Whining "if only it weren't for my birth" or "if only I were taller" provides an excuse to blame and become immobilized from attaining positive achievement. We suggest that in place of saying "if only" to yourself and other people, you face the reality of your circumstances and either work at overcoming or compromising your goals. These are much more courageous and constructive approaches to a fuller life.

Eliminate "Shoulds," "Oughts," and "Musts"

Reality is not the way we want it to be—instead, it is the way it is. Discouraged people get angry at themselves, other people, and the world because things are not the way they want. This superiority complex is best revealed by the language of discouraged people. This demand that the universe adjust itself to be convenient for the discouraged person is demonstrated by frequent use of the words *should*, *ought*, or *must*. Consider the grandiosity inherent in "should" statements:

John: It *shouldn't* be this cold in June.

Earl: People *should* eat three meals a day.

Pete: I *shouldn't* lose my car keys like this; I can't stand it.

Jane: My oil burner *shouldn't* break down; this is horrible.

Each of these "should" statements are demands that things be different from the way they in fact are. John, who complains about the cold temperature in June, expects that the universe should alter its natural conditions for him. Earl is making a universal statement about the diet of people. He is demanding that people of all nations be perhaps more like him. Pete is asking that what in fact happened, didn't happen. Jane is declaring that what occurred to her oil burner shouldn't occur. The conditions just should not have happened.

We agree that there are things we don't like and *wish* they weren't so. We would like a world where there would never be traffic jams, red lights, rejections, earthquakes, or thunderstorms. And if we were running the universe and could make these decisions, we would change all the unpleasantries of life. Then we could make things better and fairer for ourselves and others. However, we clearly recognize this as a *wish*, not a *should*. Just because we *wish* something to be doesn't mean that it *should* be. That would be a superiority complex.

Albert Ellis (1975) has pointed out that "shoulds," "oughts," and "musts" are insane. One way of becoming sane, Ellis suggests, is to "stop shoulding on yourself." Eliminate "shoulds" from your vocabulary, and use sane sentences instead. Consider our three frustrated friends—John, Earl, and Pete. They could face reality with more sane statements:

INSANE DEMANDS (DISCOURAGING)	SANE WISHES (ENCOURAGING)
John: It *shouldn't* be this cold in June.	*If I could choose, I'd rather* have warm weather. However, this weather is a fact. Just because I don't like it doesn't mean it should't be.
Earl: People *should* eat three meals a day.	In my opinion, *it would be better if* people ate three meals a day. But there is a difference between my opinion and the facts. Despite my opinion, I recognize that people have the right to eat as many or as few meals as they, not I, choose.
Pete: I *shouldn't* lose my car keys like this; I can't stand it.	I lost my car keys. I'll look for them and deal with the situation. This is an *inconvenience*, but I have no choice.

Eliminate Exaggerations

Ann: My boyfriend *slayed* me—it was *horrible,* and I just *couldn't stand it.* I could just die.

Michele: He slayed you! What do you mean?

Ann: I mean he said he didn't want to see me anymore.

Michele: Oh, and how was it horrible?

Ann: It was horrible because I need him.

Michele: It was hurtful and inconvenient, then. And what do you mean you "couldn't stand it"? You certainly seem upset, but you are standing it.

Ann: Well, I guess, but I'm really hurt.

Michele: It really is hard to lose someone. I know you'll pick up the pieces. But don't make it harder on yourself by making it a catastrophe.

Ann is exaggerating. Her misery is related to what she is telling Michele about a previous event. Ann is speaking in "can't stands" and "horribles." Naturally, by this choice of words, she is further escalating her misery. Consider these alternative ways of dealing with the situation:

EXAGGERATED LANGUAGE	RATIONAL COURAGEOUS LANGUAGE
He slayed me.	He said he didn't want to see me anymore.
It was horrible, awful, and terrible.	It was inconvenient, unfortunate, and displeasing.
I can't stand it.	I don't like it. I would prefer it otherwise if I had a choice. However, I can stand it.

Clues to Courageous Language

UNPRODUCTIVE, DISCOURAGING LANGUAGE	COURAGEOUS LANGUAGE
1. Passive and irresponsible You made me . . . The world made me . . .	*1. Active and responsible* I made myself . . . I chose to . . . I decided . . .
Add your own examples:	Add your own examples:

_____	_____
_____	_____
_____	_____

2. I can't I can't assert myself with my boss.	*2. I won't* I won't assert myself with my boss.
Add your own examples:	Add your own examples:

_____	_____
_____	_____
_____	_____

3. If only . . . , then I could If only I had better teachers then I could have gone to college.	*3. It would have been better for me if. . . . However, . . .* It would have been better for me if I had better teachers. However, I didn't, and this is where I am today. What can I do from here?

Add your own examples:

_____

_____

_____

Add your own examples:

_____

_____

_____

4. "Shoulds," "oughts," "musts"

Food is too expensive; it shouldn't cost this much.

4. I would like, or if I could choose, or it would be more convenient for me
I would like it if food didn't cost this much, and if I could choose, I would make things different.

Add your own examples:

_____

_____

_____

Add your own examples:

_____

_____

_____

5. Exaggerating language
I slipped on the dance floor in front of everyone. It was horrible, I couldn't stand it. I crawled inside myself. I'm never going to dance again.

5. Rational, factual language
I fell while I was dancing. This was an inconvenience, as I had to pick myself up. I'm going to practice my dancing skill so it doesn't happen again.

Add your own examples:

_____

_____

_____

Add your own examples:

_____

_____

_____

6. *Negative expectations*	6. *Positive expectations*
I'll try, but I know I'll never succeed.	I'm going to succeed.
There's no hope.	I'm alive and I'm going to adjust to the circumstances in the *best* way.
They won't like me.	How could they resist me?
Add your own examples:	Add your own examples:

_____   _____

_____   _____

_____   _____

7. *They say . . .*	7. *Who says? Where is the proof that they are experts? Where was their study to support their statement? Am I willing to throw my life decisions and responsibilities into their arms? How do they know?*
They say you should eat spinach.	What is the name of the person who said you should eat spinach? Where was this person's research conducted? What would be the result if I did or did not eat spinach? Can I call this person on the phone to get more information?
Etiquette dictates that you address your husband's boss's wife only by her last name until she gives you permission to do otherwise.	Who said? Why must it be? What would the results be if I didn't? How did it happen that this became the way? Why is this person's opinion more important than my opinion? Must I listen to this? Does it make sense to me?

Add some examples of your own:

_____

_____

_____

Add some examples of your own:

_____

_____

_____

8. Generalizing language
I could never . . .

I could never speak in public.

Add your own examples:

_____

_____

_____

8. Specific, factual language
In the past, I didn't seem to be able. However, if I keep plugging away, I'll increase my chances of being able to . . .
I've had a frightening time speaking in public in the past. But, doggone it, I'm going to work harder at it.

Add your own examples:

_____

_____

_____

Brush Up: Chapter 5

1. How can words arouse emotions? Give some examples of emotionally arousing sentences:

_____

_____

_____

2. What is passive language? Why is it irresponsible? Write a passive sentence, and change it to make it more active and responsible:

   Passive: _____

   Active: _____

3. What are some of the fringe benefits of speaking with "can'ts"?

4. Show how people who use "shoulds," "oughts," and "musts" are suffering from a superiority complex.

   _____

   _____

   _____

5. What kinds of more rational statements could be substituted for "shoulds," "oughts," and "musts"?

6. Why are your choices in Question 5 more rational, less insane?

7. Write a few sentences demonstrating the use of exaggerated language:

   _____

   _____

   _____

8. Why is it important to track down "who said" before building your life on "they said" statements?

9. Write a few "they said" statements that you can recall that are not accurate. Perhaps you can remember some from your childhood.

_____

_____

_____

10. With what areas of the chapter did you tend to disagree?

11. Jot in any parts of the chapter that had special meaning for you.

_____

_____

_____

12. Develop a plan for your growth of courage based upon some meaningful items in this chapter.

Developing Courageous Beliefs about Yourself, Other People, & the World

T he process of self-encouragement is complex because you, as a human being, are complex. Consequently, we have focused on developing different aspects of yourself separately. First, we discussed ways of improving your relationship with yourself through a flowing identity, self-respect, resource focusing, and enthusiasm. Next, we addressed ways of enhancing your ability to speak courageously. Now we center on approaches to developing courageous beliefs about yourself, other people, and the world.

We have suggested that the productive way to look at yourself, then, is to consider that you are the only one who is responsible for choosing whether you are your own best friend or your own worst enemy. You also are the creator of your "highs" and "lows" in life. Have you ever observed six- or seven-month-old infants trying to fulfill their hunger needs? Many children at this age attempt to put everything they see into their mouths, edible or not. Not quite sure as to where their bodies end and the rest of the world begins, however, these youngsters sometimes get themselves into trouble. As they lie on their backs, they almost inevitably observe five toes on a foot hovering above themselves. Consequently, their eager mouths send a signal to their hands to "reel in" this potential food. As they unknowingly start to bite away at their own feet, pain, with accompanying tears, develops in these helpless youngsters. Annoyed, they excitedly search for the culprit of their inconvenience. But lo and behold, they can find no external villain!

Perhaps you are not very different from a six-month-old in that at times, you are your own worst enemy. Do you continually defeat your own ends by blaming yourself or others, making excuses, apologizing for your own life, or never stopping to experience all that the world has to offer? We suggest that if you can be your own worst enemy, then, by removing some discouraging fictional beliefs, you can be your own best friend instead.

Before discussing some of these discouraging fictions and demonstrating ways of combating these unproductive beliefs, let's first consider the relationship between your fictional beliefs and emotions.

The Relationship between Beliefs and Emotions

A fiction, as you know, is a story that is not true. Sometimes it is easy to get caught up in a fictional story and to treat it as a reality. Perhaps you have some beliefs about your life that you treat as absolutely true but that are only fictions. When this occurs, you are experiencing an unproductive and distorted vision of reality similar to that of the six-month-old child.

The problem with fictions is not only that they produce an unclear reality but that they also create unproductive and crippling emotions. For example, if a little boy learns that crying every time things don't go his way makes his parents give in to him, he develops a fictional belief about life. His fiction is that he must have his own way and that if he cries or shows anger, people will give in to his wants. Of course, he will later become quite frustrated with life, because other people in the world will not respond to him as his parents did. His distorted emotions, then, are related to his mistaken belief about life.

Or imagine a little girl who complains about the fact that her sister's birthday present cost $10.00 and hers only cost $9.25. Her well-intentioned parents compensate for their "error" by giving the girl $.75, fearing a permanent scarring of her psyche. This little girl is in the process of developing a fictional belief that the world is fair and just. Again, frustration is likely to set in, since there will be many times in her life when her fictions of justice will not be fulfilled. Both these children are not being taught to respect reality.

Emotions, then, are the result of beliefs about life. As we suggested before, psychologists speak of people who are emotionally disturbed; another way to express this is to refer to them as being "disturbed in their beliefs." Beliefs are the ways in which people look at themselves, others, and the world. Of course, if their beliefs are crooked, then so will their emotions be inappropriate. These emotions are, nevertheless, consistent with the personal beliefs, or what Adler called "private logic," of the disturbed thinker.

For example, a person who looks at the world with suspicion may believe that everyone is out to get him. When he observes two people at a bus stop in their everyday casual conversation, he may believe that they are plotting to kill him. Depending upon how seriously disturbed his beliefs are, he might even attempt to harm them in self-defense before they can get him. His fears, suspicions, and actions certainly make sense out of the way he is looking at life and his fictional belief system. His emotion (perhaps fear) may provide the energy to propel him in service of his beliefs. The illustration shows how your beliefs, emotions, and actions work together in service of each other—and your stated or unrealized goals.

Your emotions are the servants to your beliefs.

As long as people's beliefs are accurate and coincide relatively well with universal reality, so will their emotions and actions be

appropriate. Consequently, people who perceive accurately are more likely to be congruent and successful in reaching their goals. Accurately perceiving people have overcome Error I—the error of disrespecting reality.

Emotions are natural and genuine consequences of beliefs; they are not to be denied or treated lightly. Many theories currently address this relationship between thinking, feeling, and acting. Carl Rogers (1961), for example, suggests that one way of helping people is through dealing with their emotions as opposed to dealing with their beliefs or actions. And it has been demonstrated that allowing people to express their emotions in a safe, accepting relationship helps their beliefs to change anyway. Our belief is that although this approach is certainly valid, it may not be the most efficient way of producing change.

William Glasser (1975) and B. F. Skinner (1973), on the other hand, suggest approaching people's beliefs and feelings by focusing on their behavior first. Not placing emphasis on the way people think or feel, reality therapy and behavior therapy focus on action or behaving. Again, both approaches have demonstrated successes. Our approach here, however, suggests that the alteration of a behavior only changes that behavior, with perhaps slight generalizing effect on other behaviors. Albert Ellis (1962) notes, however, that by modifying one belief, people change, many, many behaviors. So, we are nourishing the notion that changing your discouraging beliefs is the most efficient way of altering your feelings and behaviors, hence your total self.

Are we suggesting, then, that people create their own emotional disturbance, discouragement, and inaction through their beliefs? Absolutely! Try a few examples to demonstrate the powerful role that beliefs play in your life.

IMAGINATION EXERCISE 1

Think of the most embarrassing moment you have ever experienced. Carefully explore the details of the occasion. Imagine what the other people around you thought of you. Take a few minutes. Jot in a few comments about the occasion, including your feelings.

_____

_____

_____

Assuming that you are not embarrassed prior to the exercise, did you find yourself becoming somewhat embarrassed while you were thinking? If so, you have watched yourself orchestrate an emotion.

IMAGINATION EXERCISE 2

Think about all the misery in the world today. The unfairness, the diseases, the violence, the crooked politicians, the child abusers, etc. Add to this list some pet peeves of your own. What about the belief that it is unfair that some people are filthy rich while others have to work very hard just to survive?

_____

_____

_____

How do these pet peeves make you feel?

_____

_____

_____

Again, if you found that you could make yourself feel a little annoyed, angry, or even depressed, you have successfully created these emotions by what you focused on. You talked yourself into this misery.

Although you could go on demonstrating to yourself how emo-

114

tions are caused, it would be more productive at this point to take a look at some fictional beliefs people have that discourage them from reaching their goals. The discussions of these fictions are largely based on the writings of Albert Ellis (1962); they are somewhat expanded here for relevance to this book. They are by no means all-encompassing of fictional beliefs, and it would be a very good idea to develop an awareness of some of your own fictional beliefs while attacking them (with a sense of humor).

Magical Fiction

DISCOURAGING FICTION

"There is magic in the world to help me reach my goals without full effort on my part." By just sitting back and hoping that your goals will arrive on your doorstep, you are doomed to not achieving them. *There exists no Santa Claus or Tooth Fairy!* Most readers would, no doubt, agree. Yet remnants of beliefs in these fictional characteristics are evident in many people's everyday behaviors. Consider the following believers in magic.

EXAMPLE 1

Sharon, sixty pounds overweight and committed to a goal of losing weight, goes over to her friend's house for dinner. Sharon knows her friend is an expert in Italian cooking. As she stares at the lasagna dinner in front of her, she says (with a magic wand and a puff of smoke), "Oh well, how much can one meal affect me anyway? I wouldn't want to offend her."

> By just sitting back and hoping that your goals will arrive on your doorstep with the morning paper, you are doomed to not achieving them. There exists no Santa Claus or Tooth Fairy.

Sharon's fiction is that there is magic in the world; its trick will be to allow the lasagna to pass secretly through her body without registering the calories. She believes she can defy the physical laws of nature. At this moment, perhaps she is demonstrating nothing different from a belief in Santa Claus. She is disrespecting reality.

EXAMPLE 2

Leroy decides to park illegally and assumes that no one will notice it. After all, there were no other spaces around, and he'll only be going to one store, and it won't take long.

Leroy's fiction is that someone (perhaps a tooth fairy whose work is primarily carried on in the evenings) will be available to shelter his car magically during the day.

EXAMPLE 3

Joe, 54, continues smoking excessively despite the warnings from the U.S. Surgeon General on the hazards of this practice. Joe says, "I knew somebody who smoked every day for over 50 years who lived to be 97. That stuff is a bunch of hogwash."

Joe's fictional belief is that he has a magical immunity to the laws of the universe. Perhaps he can defy gravity and fly by himself as well!

These people, and many like them, refuse to face and accept reality head-on. In this refusal, people blindly destroy their own ends, assuming that some magic exists beyond themselves to help them reach their goals. Three kinds of *magic seekers* are discussed here: (1) the *superstitious ones*; (2) the *passive waiters*; and (3) the *I-want-what-I-want-now people*.

SUPERSTITIOUS ONES

Superstitious ones are individuals who use fate, the stars, black cats, ladders, etc., to explain their lives. Despite the fact that many people cling to these notions, there has not been one single bit of scientific evidence to indicate that superstitions play any role in people's lives except through self-fulfilling prophecy. If people come to expect that a horrible thing is going to happen to them, they focus on all the negative possibilities that day, and sure enough, something negative will happen. That it has been *expected* will emphasize its importance.

Consider the logical absurdity of superstitions. People who believe, for example, that walking under a ladder causes bad luck are suggesting that there is some "force" that will be annoyed by their defiant behavior and will retaliate.

IMAGINATION EXERCISE

If the ladder superstition is true, then somewhere there must be a giant computer from which every individual in the universe is being constantly monitored for things like walking under ladders, etc. When an individual, then, living in a given city, say Boise, Idaho, walks under a ladder, the monitor representative of that region is called into action. This representative's job is to cause some unfortunate happening. Consider how many times this goes on in the course of a day in a world of four billion plus. What a monumental task for the people in the computer room! And if you think that this is difficult and demanding, imagine how busy these monitors are every Friday the 13th!

If people come to believe a superstition and expect a horrible thing to happen to them, they focus on a possible negative happening, and sure enough, that's exactly what they will see.

ATTACKING EXERCISE

Imagine at this moment that you are a very important person and that people everywhere know you, and many of them are out to get you. Hop in your car, and drive a few blocks. Look through your rearview mirror at the car following you. Watch how long the driver follows you. When you turn and this person doesn't, see if someone else picks up. Get out of your car, and start walking where there are other people. Watch how shrewd some people are at pretending they aren't looking at you while you just know they are monitoring your every move. Say hello to a few people, and watch their reactions.

If you really got into this attacking exercise and put on the glasses of a grandiose and persecuted suspicious person, you experienced some strange sensations. When your mind was set to look at the world as being a dangerous place, your emotions were affected. Perhaps you experienced fear in this example. Your *beliefs* affected the way you felt and acted toward others. You probably even looked different to people, and they consequently responded to this suspicious-looking you.

When you believe superstitions, you look at the world in a distorted way. When our friend from Boise walked under the ladder, then, because of his *beliefs* about its effects, he began *focusing* on the bad events of the day. He was sure to find some!

There is a joke about two boys—one an optimist, one a pessimist. The pessimist, who *focused* on only the bad, was put into a room full of all the finest toys. There were skateboards, scooters, construction blocks, everything. As this pessimistic child walked into the room, he became frightened. Seeing only the negative, he started to cry, saying, "If I start to play with any of these, I'm liable to break them and really get into trouble."

In the room next door, the optimistic child opened the door and, instead of beautiful toys, was greeted by a huge pile of manure. The *positive-focusing* youngster, with eyes beaming excitedly, jubilantly yelled, "Oh boy, with all this around, there must be a pony somewhere!"

The second youngster had himself set to see positives, whereas the first child was set to see only negatives. Regardless of what circumstances they were exposed to, the way they *focused* determined their *beliefs*, *feelings*, and *actions*.

Thus you see the effects of the way you view your superstitions. When you cease to give meaning to these empty rituals, they lose control over you. Remember, the first step in living life more fully is to take charge of it.

Now do the previous attacking exercise again. As you drive your car and walk down the main street of your town, say to yourself, "I do not have a superiority complex. I'm not so important that the people in the world are going to go out of their way to follow me. They have lives of their own to be concerned about." Did you feel different? If so, you have witnessed the power of dispelling magical beliefs and have taken over more control of your life.

ATTACKING EXERCISE

Courageously challenge your most crippling superstition. For example, walk under as many ladders as you can find. Put a ladder up and walk under it over and over again. As you are doing so, say to yourself. "Isn't it absurd that I would believe this nonsense?" After you complete this, say to yourself, "I'm going to make this a new and good day." *Focus* on the positives. And congratulate yourself. You are taking more control over your life.

Superstitious ones blame their good and bad days on things external to themselves. They buy the S→R model of understanding themselves. When they are able to combat these fictions courageously, they realize a sense of control, freedom, and active responsibility for their lives. Superstitious ones are similar to the second type of magic seekers—the *passive waiters*. Both types feel helpless in the throes of more powerful controls.

PASSIVE WAITERS

Joe: You didn't tell me that you won $10,000 in the lottery!

Bill: You didn't ask.

The passive waiters helplessly wait for magic to force others to ask them the right question, notice them, approve or disapprove of them, and so on. Of course, this is a comfortable way of life, since there are minimal risks involved. If you never try to get your fair share, no one will get angry with you or be annoyed with you. By not taking initiative in your life, you will never be accused of doing anything wrong.

Jane (disgruntled): Huh, I saw Eleanor in town, and she walked right by me, not even having the courtesy to say hello!

Sally: Oh my, what did you say to her?

Jane: Nothing—I was waiting for her to talk first.

Sally: Maybe she felt the same way.

Passive waiters believe that someone else "has the magic" and consequently is responsible for initiating involvements, conversations, etc.

If you feel that you are a passive waiter in some aspects of your life, think of some of the fringe benefits of this choice of life-style. Jot them in below.

_____

_____

_____

If you were able to demonstrate to yourself the rewards of this form of believing in magic, you are becoming well aware of why passivity is so hard to change. Nevertheless, with some courage, try an attacking exercise to dispel this fiction and to get more control over your life and goals.

ATTACKING EXERCISE

Consider some things in your life that you *want* and believe you have the right to have but have lacked some courage to go after. Consider as well something that you have held back going after, half believing that somehow or other, if you waited, it would magically happen. Remember Chapters 1 and 2 (the unproductive vs. the courageous view)? How might you take responsibility for achieving the courageous view? Set up some steps that you might actively take to reach this goal. Consider: When will I take my first step? How will I achieve this goal? Set up a date by which you will have your effort achieved. Mark it off on a calendar. Feel good, because again you are slowly removing some of those crippling controls over your life that once rendered you helpless.

You probably are finding, if you are following through on these attacking exercises, that *there is magic in the world—but the magic is within you.*

There is no magic in the world outside of you—only the magic within you—the untapped possibilities.

I-WANT-WHAT-I-WANT-RIGHT-NOW PEOPLE

There are people who believe that they can have what they want when they want it (to buy everything in sight and still have money). We refer to these people as the *I-want-what-I-want-right-now* magic seekers.

Give the following problem to an eighteen-month-old child: "You can have this cone of ice cream right now or $1,000 tomorrow. You cannot have both." Which would you guess most eighteen-month-old children would choose?

We believe that the young child would choose the ice cream. Why? Most likely, because children are more interested in immediate satisfaction. When people mature, they slowly develop an ability to defer immediate satisfaction and can wait for long-range, bigger satisfactions. This maturity is an important dimension of achieving goals.

The well-intentioned yet unsuccessful dieter, for example, wakes up each day determined. Yet when the true test appears, this person succumbs to magical belief. By eating and eating, this individual satisfies temporary, short-range needs—like the eighteen-month-old child. However, the dieter loses sight of the important long-range goal. So the person experiences short-range rewards but regrets it over and over again when getting on the scale. An attacking exercise here, taken seriously, can dispel the notion that you can have your cake and eat it too.

ATTACKING EXERCISE

Think of a goal that you want and that you would be willing to work on. Make sure it is one that, for some reason or other, you haven't achieved because of some short-range needs on your part interfering. Become determined, taking full responsibility for your actions, so that the next time you get the opportunity, you won't cop out by succumbing to the short-range need. When will you have the opportunity to challenge it? What will you tell yourself that will help you get over the hump? Take pride in your newly found courage!

Long-range goal (stated goal)

Short-range interference (unrealized goal)

_____

When is the showdown?

_____

Dealing with your fictions was probably painful. As you become aware of your possibilities, you may have a tendency to try to run away from them. After all, if you believed that there was magic in the world, then something else was responsible for your happiness. Consequently, this something else was also responsible for your reaching your goals. Here are a few other attacking exercises to meet reality head-on:

ATTACKING EXERCISE

What in your life is a real concern that you have not faced? Why? What can you do about it? When will you do it? What would be a good first step? When will you take it?

What are you going to face that you avoided until now?

_____

_____

Make a plan to face the problem.

_____

_____

Write in date and time.

_____

ATTACKING EXERCISE

Where are you undershooting your possibilities? Would you like to get closer to your fuller possibilities? How could you start? What are your assets that can help lead you there? Who is responsible for you to get there? Mark your calendar. Make a commitment.

Make some constructive notes for yourself that you will return to later.

_____

_____

_____

ATTACKING EXERCISE

Can you think of a person whom you care for but have not told? Why? Do you want to change that? Can you? If you only had twenty-four hours to live, could you change that? If you make a commitment, when will you start? How will you go about it? Who is responsible for it?

With whom will you be more honest?

_____

What will you tell this person?

_____

When? Set up a date and time.

_____

Feel that sense of satisfaction when you accomplish your task!

ATTACKING EXERCISE

Write down an area of your life in which you function under each of these four categories: "I can't," "I won't," "I can," "I will." Which one would you like to change the most? Can you move to the next step? When will you start? Can you change any other? When will you start?

You have been experiencing some difficult times, no doubt, reading this chapter. There is no magic outside of you, and when you face reality, it is painful. But we trust you have experienced a surge of accomplishment or mastery along the way. Have you been in touch with your own personal responsibility in achieving your goals? *Congratulate yourself!* You are in a rare minority! Keep your progress in mind, focusing on your efforts, not your fears. Now— progress courageously to overcoming the perfection fiction once and for all.

Perfection Fiction

"If I expose a personal weakness or imperfection, you would think less of me, and then I would be less worthwhile." This is a common perfection fiction. Rudolf Dreikurs, world-renowned psychiatrist, suggested that one of the greatest attributes a human being can have is the "courage to be imperfect." Why did Dreikurs place such an emphasis on imperfection? It's easy to see when you think of it. Most of the time that people do not grow, move ahead, or make changes in their lives, it is because of their fear of failure or of not being perfect. How many things would you like to do in your one lifetime that you hold yourself back from, because you are afraid of making a mistake or looking bad? When people develop the courage of imperfection, a whole new life of unlimited possibilities opens up to them.

Take another look at the Courage Direction Chart:

I can't make an effort.	→	I won't make an effort.	→	I can make an effort.	→	I will and am making an effort.
Desire for mastery of sameness						Desire for mastery of newness (courage of imperfection)
Helpless						Responsible
Opinionated						Open, flexible

When people are turned off and discouraged, their possibilities are narrowed, and they feel helpless. They seek perfection in everything they do. Unfortunately, because of this desire, they don't do much! They feel that they *can't* make an effort to develop new behaviors and habits. What if they tried something new and failed? As people move to the right on the Courage Direction Chart, they courageously start to take risks, to grow, and to desire newness in each of their 25,600 days. They are more willing to risk uncertainty as they develop the courage to be imperfect.

ATTACKING EXERCISE

Think for a few moments how your life would be different if you started immediately to work at overcoming fear of failure. Imagine that you would never again be afraid of being imperfect or looking silly, or even of being rejected or criticized. How would your life be different? Jot down a few examples below of things that you would do if you totally—and I mean totally—had the courage to be imperfect. Write whatever you bring into your mind. No holds barred!

_____

_____

_____

People with overwhelming needs to do everything perfectly are trying to cover up all potential sources of weakness. Their greatest concern is that they may fail and look bad. Consequently, perfectionists plan every detail, sometimes for months ahead. They lose their spontaneity, and they panic when something unexpected happens. As children, they often were invited to believe that they were worthwhile only when they succeeded. Their parents may have been extremely concerned with performance, and their little perfectionists incorporated unrealistically high standards.

Would you rather live an "imperfectly full" or a "perfectly empty" life?

Perfectionists are their own worst enemies. They believe that unless they are faultless, they are worthless. They have a difficult time keeping up with their self-expectations. Sometimes they deliberately set their goals low to avoid failing. When they are in new situations, they become frightened about the possibility that they may make a mistake, and if they do, they live it over and over again mentally. A need for safety, security, and predictability becomes predominant for these discouraged people.

ATTACKING EXERCISE
   Consider the following aspects of your life, and ask yourself whether you have undershot your possibilities out of fear of failure and perfection needs. Define your ultimate dream in each category:

Your career _____

Your educational level _____

Your romantic life _____

Your daily life—how different is one day from another, or are they all the same? _____

_____

If you are unhappy or dissatisfied about any of these or other aspects of your life because you have undershot your possibilities, perhaps you are one of the following types of perfectionists: (1) *the compulsive-planning-to-the-detail people*, (2) *the if-I-don't-try-I-can't-fail people*, and (3) *the every-hair-neatly-in-place people*.

Perfectionists are their own worst enemies. They believe that unless they are faultless, they are worthless. Sometimes they deliberately set their goals low to avoid failing.

COMPULSIVE-PLANNING-TO-THE-DETAIL PEOPLE

Bob wakes up every day at exactly 7:50, brushes his teeth (same number of strokes each day), washes and dries in the same routine way every day, and completes these tasks at exactly 8:25. He eats a breakfast that he plans a week in advance and drives to work exactly the same way every day (it takes exactly 16 minutes). He is twenty-six years old now and says that he will work with his present company for exactly seven years, and at that point, at age thirty-three, he will get married to a girl he will meet when he is thirty-one. Right now he is saving exactly $200 a month, and he needs exactly $15,000 in order to have enough financial security for mar-

riage. He even knows what color hair and how much educa-
tion his wife, when he meets her at age thirty-one, will have.

Bob is a compulsive planner perfectionist. He has lost all spontaneity in life and is governed by a prescribed routine. As long as the
routine falls into place, Bob is okay, but watch out when something
unforeseen occurs—*panic!*

Bob has organized his life into a safe, predictable existence that
he has mastered. He is unwilling, even frightened, to break the
routine and do something new. He is paralyzed by fear of imperfection. Before Bob takes a chance and goes skiing, for example, he
will plan on taking lessons two years ahead, will take lessons for two
more years, and finally will take that first slope. Rest assured that
when he does descend his first slope, he will be one of the best, and
no youngster is going to see Bob fall! However, there is a good
chance that the first slope will never arrive.

ATTACKING EXERCISE

If you experience a need to detail compulsively every aspect
of your life, start slowly to develop the courage to be spontane-
ous. One day in the near future, wake up, skip work if it is a
workday, take off, and do something you have always wanted
but were afraid to do. (This is one exercise you cannot plan!)

ATTACKING EXERCISE

Consider someone you would like to be with but were always afraid would reject you. Call that person up and make
arrangements to go out tonight.

Who? _____

Where will you ask this person to go? _____

_____

When will you call? _____

IF-I-DON'T-TRY-I-CAN'T-FAIL PEOPLE

Mrs. R. noticed that during history class, Billy rarely handed in anything written on his paper but his name. Occasionally he would write obviously wrong responses. One day he wrote that Dr. J (the basketball player) was the first president of the United States. After much counseling, Billy said, "As long as I don't write anything, the teacher will think I'm just being a smart aleck, and I could always act as though if I wanted to, I could give the right answer. But what if I try and don't get it right? That would be really bad. I'd sure rather be called a bad kid than be called stupid."

Billy is suffering from perfectionism or the lack of courage to be imperfect. You can see how this serves his purpose. Never will his weakness become apparent to people, because he never participates. Of course, his strengths will never become apparent either. He fantasizes to himself that he always could succeed if he wanted. Underneath he lacks the courage to move.

Dan and Dave, two college sophomores, were friends who were quite the opposite in perfection styles. Wherever Dan went, he would strike up a conversation with a girl and would soon be asking her out on a date. Dave was fascinated by Dan's courage, and even though the girl would often flatly turn down Dan's request, he had his share of successes.

Dave rarely took a risk. Before he would ask a girl out, he would plan for months, study her likes and dislikes, rehearse the things he would say to her, and finally go. His reward was that he minimized his chances of being rejected. He had an almost perfectly clean slate, but he seldom went out.

It was on Saturday nights, when Dave was sitting home by himself and Dan was out enjoying himself, that Dave wondered whether his "safe" style was really productive.

One lifetime to do it in, right? When Dave asked Dan how he

felt about the rejections, Dan replied, "Oh, I learn from my rejections how to improve my approach!" As Alfred Adler, the prominent Viennese psychiatrist, suggested, "life is the process of making big errors smaller ones."

ATTACKING EXERCISE

Remembering the phrase "life is the process of making big errors smaller ones," in which aspect of your life can you decrease your amount of error? Choose an aspect that you would like to change, live more fully in, and be willing to change.

_____

_____

_____

ATTACKING EXERCISE

Reread the first story of little Billy. Does that remind you of yourself in any way? Are there areas of your life where you have adopted the attitude that if you don't try, you can't fail? Ask yourself, "How much would failure really cost?" What can you do about it? When will you start? Make a commitment.

Area of your life. _____

What would be the worst possible cost of failure? _____

_____

What can you do to change? _____

_____

Give a date and time for your change. _____

ink of an aspect of your life as you reread the story of Dan Dave. If that is Dave on the left and Dan on the right, where would you put yourself in this aspect? Draw yourself in at that spot. How could you go above moving closer to Dan? When will you start? Make a commitment.

Adler suggested that "life is a process of making big errors smaller ones."

EVERY-HAIR-NEATLY-IN-PLACE PEOPLE

Sally and Jim keep the most perfectly spotless house that you could imagine. Part of their emphasis on cleanliness perhaps was influenced by the TV commercials where friends visit and disapprovingly wrinkle their noses at the cigar smoke or the spotted water glasses. They are determined that this will never happen to them. You will notice that if your visit to their house is unplanned, they won't open the door out of fear of exposing their imperfection. You may also notice a great deal of personal discomfort while you are there, since you are afraid of getting anything dirty.

Elaine and Harold's house, on the other hand, reflects a relaxed atmosphere where you can go in, sit on the floor if you choose, and need not even feel guilty about going to their bathroom. Like Dan in the previous example, they are not concerned with perfection or looking good. They are, rather, interested in living and enjoying life. They do not feel that their worth is based on how their house looks to other people.

Sally and Jim are perfectionists. They are extremely concerned about exposing a weakness or an imperfection and believe that you will think less of them if you see "how they really are." It requires a great deal of energy to keep up this image. They spend most of their lives apologizing for it, and perhaps you find that it is difficult for you to feel comfortable around them.

Certainly you have met people who can't be out in public unless they are perfect. Every hair must be neatly in place, and their clothing must be perfectly matched. The person with the courage to be imperfect feels natural in the world and needs no gimmicks to be okay.

An interesting fringe benefit occurs when you develop the courage to be yourself, the way you really are, with people. That is, other people can start to be their real selves, and they have less of a need to be phony around you. Relationships improve as you wave goodbye forever to the facades.

ATTACKING EXERCISE

Where are you "not yourself"? Where you feel uncomfortable and feel a need to look perfect, to act perfectly, or to be perfectly well dressed? Consider the consequences of this stifling behavior. How can you attack these needs? This, of course, does not mean becoming a slob but rather becoming the person you feel like being. When will you try it?

Where is a stifling situation?   _____

_____

What can you do to overcome your feelings of intimidation?   _____

_____

Give a date and time that you will try.   _____

_____

Highly influenced by fictions, this area of your life is sometimes difficult to overcome. Perhaps you have heard the saying that "cleanliness is next to godliness." Ask yourself, "Who said?" "Why is it thus?" "Is this phrase relevant for me and my life?" "Where is the research that proves this?" Of course, there is no research that proves this. It is a fiction, and any time you base your life on fictions, you are living in a fictional world.

One final note: One of the ways of judging your personal growth is in measuring your willingness to try new experiences and to take risks in life.

THINGS TO REMEMBER ABOUT ATTACKING PERFECTION FICTIONS

1. Refer to the Courage Direction Chart on page 126. Where are you on this chart concerning different areas of your life? Consider the attacking exercises in this chapter to move to the right-hand side.

2. Remember the story of Dave and Dan. How can you become more like Dan?

3. Remember that you have only one life to live—if you don't do it now, when will you?

4. Consider the following ways of viewing life:

Failure is only a suggestion that there was a better alternative.

Life is the process of making big errors smaller ones.

When you show people your natural imperfections, they feel more at ease with you, and the relationship is likely to improve.

The most important ingredient to have to enjoy life fully is the "courage to be imperfect."

ATTACKING EXERCISE

Take five minutes, review this very important category, and when completed, *try this: Imagine* that your doctor has just told you that you only have twenty-four hours to live. Tomorrow at this time, your one life will cease. Take a few minutes now to consider how you are going to live those twenty-four hours. What will you do? When you are satisfied that you have established a plan, jot it in below. If possible, share your experience with someone.

_____

_____

_____

What kinds of things were important to you? What did you choose to do? Did you have any regrets about life? Did you wish that you could have had more time? Did you want to tell someone something that you lacked the courage to say before? Address any question that is relevant to you:

_____

_____

_____

Imagine that your doctor has just informed you it is not true and that you probably have many, many more years of your natural life to live. Hearing this, you may feel a sense of refreshment. A full lifetime is ahead of you. What will you do with it?

Consider your experience in this exercise and the major points of this chapter together. How do they fit into making your life more courageous? At this moment, jot in any comments you have:

_____

_____

_____

Complaining Fiction

Wife to Husband: What do you think of this! I ordered filet, and they brought me sirloin instead. They can't even get an order right and at these prices yet!

Husband: Let's tell the waiter.

Wife: No, no, let it go!

"If I complain to myself without action it will change my life." How much complaining like this do you hear during the course of a day? On the job, at home, on the street, in restaurants—it's always so easy to find dissatisfied people. Yet most of these people refuse to take personal responsibility for their complaints. They would prefer to drag themselves (and others around them) down. Complaining about the unfair treatment in their lives without taking action affords them an easy way out.

ATTACKING EXERCISE
Think about a pet complaint of yours that you have not actively addressed, and jot it down:

_____

_____

_____

You found yourself going around and around in circles, complaining and complaining. Perhaps you became caught up in a quicksand of negativism, with no change in your life (except increased unhappiness). Consider some fringe benefits of the complaining-without-doing life-style. Write them in below:

_____

_____

_____

You could have included many advantages of complaining without action. Perhaps you suggested that there are no risks; such behavior may provide good excuses for unproductivity and immobility.

But take your complaint one step further. Instead of the vicious cycle, make a responsible decision about the disposition of your complaint. Bring it to the crossroad! Choose between action and acceptance!

Consider which of these two courses of action is more appropriate for your complaint. If you decide that you want to take responsible action, (1) consider the risks; (2) consider the amount of time and energy you may need to invest; (3) plan a step-by-step approach, with times and dates you hope to accomplish these steps; and (4) move.

If your decision is to accept the problem, (1) stop complaining, since you are only dragging yourself down; (2) accept the problem as a new part of your reality; and (3) move on to new concerns that you can have a higher probability of improving.

Bring your complaint to the crossroad—action or acceptance.

You may need to remind yourself continually of this crossroads approach to deal with your complaints.

ATTACKING EXERCISE

Attack a few common complaints of your life via the crossroads approach. After doing so, experience again that responsible feeling of getting a greater hold on your life and the things you once allowed to immobilize and stifle you.

Environmental Fiction

"My environment made me be the way I am today." It is so commonly accepted that people are products of their environment that it almost seems absurd to dispute it. After all, can't statistics be found to show how difficult it is for poor people to improve their lot? And many churches will even claim that if they can influence a child with their philosophy for the first few years of life, they will keep that child as a lifetime member. And very few people will dispute the belief that many mannerisms—such as the way people hold a fork, the way they walk, etc.—are related to early childhood conditioning.

So strong are these notions that two of the major forces in psychology—psychoanalysis and behaviorism—rest their reputations on these beliefs.

Psychoanalysts even attempt to reconstruct early childhood experiences to show patients how their present lives are just reenactments of early experiences. Even their research points out the effects of parenting patterns on children's development.

Behaviorists take the position that behavior is the result of previous environmental rewards and punishments. Optimistically, however, behaviorists grant that behavior changes as rewards and punishments change. For people to change, according to psychoanalytic theory, however, they should experience a form of therapy whereby their unconscious motivations are brought into consciousness with the aid of analysts.

No attempt is made to argue against the practice of either approach. Both systems find success in their treatment of problems.

And we believe that future ideas about therapy will take a direction in which both approaches will be incorporated with self-encouragement.

However, self-encouragement is a movement-oriented therapy that attempts to view people as active, goal-directed individuals who create their own discouragement, defeats, and symptoms. The difference lies largely in the fact that psychoanalysis and behaviorism tend to be S→R, and self-encouragement is S→You→R. Remember from Chapter 1—we suggested that the productive way to view yourself is to take responsibility and not to become a blamer of your parents, environment, and so forth.

Granted, it is true that behavioral science research has found trends to demonstrate that certain environmental patterns lead to certain personality problems, emotional disturbances, etc. But not one single study has demonstrated a *perfect* relationship between early environment and later development. Yes, that's right! Not one single study.

So although we would be the first to agree that environment invites certain behavioral patterns, we would also be first to disagree that environment completely controls human behavior. Going one step further, we would like to demonstrate that believing this fiction has the practical effect of limiting your possibilities. Again, as the section on superstitions demonstrated, by using your environment as an excuse for lack of performance, you are crippling yourself. After all, if you can't do something because you were criticized and even treated harshly in your home, you have an excuse not to grow today.

Consider these two examples of people who use the environmental fiction. As you are reading them, think to yourself—*what are the fringe benefits of believing as this person does?*

EXAMPLE 1

Colleen, 23, says she stays away from men because her mother always made her feel that if she didn't act like a perfect lady in their presence, they would talk about her later. She became extremely self-conscious and felt that because she wasn't feminine enough, there was no hope for her in her relationships with men.

EXAMPLE 2

Susie, 45, says that she eats a lot of food today, especially sweets, because she was rewarded with sweets as a child. Every time she did something that her parents liked, they gave her sweets.

Both persons, remember, are brilliant and possibly even have accurate insights. And we do believe that their patterns will be hard to break. Why? Because of past conditioning? Perhaps, since habits of thinking or acting are difficult to change. But even more importantly, they will be difficult to change because they are safe and rewarding to these individuals. After all, Colleen doesn't have to face dates and possible rejections because of her environmental fiction, and Susie can continue eating because of hers. Yet we know that in the long run, both will fail to reach their stated goals as long as they continue to believe these notions.

CHANGING YOUR PRESENT
WILL SOON CHANGE YOUR PAST

If you accept every single environmental invitation, your environment totally determines your behavior. It will continue to rule you until you come to the realization that you can rise above it and say no. You, and only you, can be responsible for that choice. It is quite easy to fall back on the environmental excuse and not reach your goals. We would even agree that it is harder for some people than others to reach their goals because of past environmental experiences. But remember, as you claim to be a product of your environmental experience and your past—your present choices will someday form a part of your past!

Think about it. If you truly believe that your past environment affects your development, and if you agree that your present decisions will soon be part of your influential past, then a positive decision made now will make it easier for you in the future. *You can create a healthier past in your future by changing your present.*

Three Insights

Albert Ellis (1975) suggests that three insights about the present–past relationship are essential to people's growth. Insight 1 is the knowledge that certain antecedent conditions have caused your present problems. Many people do recognize that there are causes for present behavior. The discouraged, helpless person understands only this insight.

> If you claim that you are a product of your past, your choices today will form part of your past tomorrow.

Insight 2 is the understanding that the conditions that occur to people early in life continue to affect them mainly because people still choose to be affected by them. It is at this point that people begin to recognize that the cause for present behavior is not automatically the past but what they keep telling themselves about that past.

Insight 3 is recognizing Insights 1 and 2 and becoming determined to work at removing any problems. When people experience this insight, they become more S→You→R in their philosophy of life, thereby taking responsible actions to change.

REMOVE YOUR PAST IDENTITIES

Clients often say, "This is the kind of person I am." This statement suggests they have identities carved in granite, as we suggested in Chapter 3, with a helpless inability to change. Self-encouraged people do not have the same dogmatic certainty about themselves. They see themselves as exciting, changing people who look more like moving, flowing rivers than stone structures.

ATTACKING EXERCISE
What kinds of identities do you have of yourself? Jot down in each of the columns below at least three things about yourself that fit into each column. The first column (*solid*) suggests that you believe this characteristic is too crystallized to change. The second column (*liquid*) suggests that this is fairly characteristic of you but could change with a great degree of effort. The third column (*gas*) suggests those characteristics you would have very little difficulty changing.

ME—SOLID   ME—LIQUID   ME—GAS

_____   _____   _____

_____   _____   _____

_____   _____   _____

Choose one in each column that you will no longer accept as a reality. Ask yourself, "How would my life be different if this were no longer true of me?" Now, courageously think of a time when you will have an opportunity to demonstrate to yourself that this trait is no longer you.

EXAMPLE

John can't speak up in restaurants when he is served food that tastes terrible. He might explain this on the basis that he grew up in a home where "children were seen but not heard." Perhaps he was even punished every time he was assertive. John might have placed "timid" in the solid or liquid column. In order to attack this past identity and put it in its place, he might wait until he gets a poorly cooked meal again and turn it back. Try the same. Make a commitment. When will you prove to yourself that you have been living an environmental fiction?

Now we ask you: Which is more productive—for John to spend his energies continually blaming his mother or for John to move onward, courageously challenging his past identities? We think the latter. If you agree and are finding yourself willing to change some of your environmental fictions, you are becoming a self-determined rather than an environmentally determined person. And while the behaviorists and analysts keep demonstrating that perhaps some 30 percent of the people who experience a certain environment will act in a certain way, proudly place yourself in the self-determined category. The sky has become your limit as you shed the shells of environmental fictions.

ATTACKING EXERCISE

Work at sensitively recognizing times when you think or say something suggesting that you are the way you are today because of your environment. Stop yourself and ask, "How can I reword that sentence so that I take responsibility for myself and not blame my past?"

ENVIRONMENTAL FICTION	ENVIRONMENTAL AND PERSONAL FACT
I hated school because of my teachers.	I hated school because of the way I looked at my teachers.

143

Notice the personal responsibility in the right-hand example. Construct some of your typical environmental fictions, and then reconstruct them to take more responsibility for them.

| | ENVIRONMENTAL AND |
ENVIRONMENTAL FICTION	PERSONAL FACT
_____ _____	_____
_____	_____
_____	_____

ATTACKING EXERCISE

Encourage yourself to become aware of some of your environmental fictions, and every time you find yourself using them as an excuse, say to yourself *"I'm having a relapse.* How can I go about thinking and speaking and behaving more responsibly?"

Blaming Fiction

"My misery is caused externally (by other people and the world)." When you become more fully in touch with the realities of your world, you rely less on magic and hope and more on yourself. This makes you a more active, involved human being, seeking your life goals in a more responsible way.

Along with forever eliminating the magic fiction comes the powerful realization that ultimately you are the creator of the way you *choose* to look at your life. We agree that there do exist many, many events in the world over which you have little or no control. This is reality. But remember from Chapter 1: It is the way you look at that reality that affects you, not the way reality is.

IMAGINATION EXERCISE

Do you know someone who seems to have everything going for him or her in life but is still unhappy? Describe this person.

_____

_____

IMAGINATION EXERCISE

Do you know anyone who has experienced a great deal of misfortune in life but is still a great inspiration to you and others? Describe this person.

_____

_____

IMAGINATION EXERCISE

Do you know someone who makes a catastrophe out of everything, even the smallest misfortune? Describe this person.

_____

_____

Why is it that some people can handle a great deal of stress and tension in life whereas others have difficulty with the slightest inconvenience? It would be absurd to suggest that external events automatically cause the response (S→R) if you were able to give examples in these imagination exercises. A more sensible explanation is one suggesting that each person views events differently. We believe, again, that it is the way you look at the world that affects you, not the way the world is (S→You→R). Then consider your misery. Is it automatically created by the things that happen to *you*, or do you *choose* to create misery by the way you look at your world?

ATTACKING EXERCISE

Consider a recent setback you've experienced in life that you say made you miserable. Did the setback *automatically* make you miserable, or did you play a role in making it worse? Now—consider accepting reality (no magic), and find other ways of looking at this event. How many different ways can you view the happening? Write them in below:

_____

_____

_____

What you have done is break the chain from the stimulus to the response. You have created for yourself an alternate way of viewing and responding to your situation.

Brush Up: Chapter 6

1. What does "your emotions are the servants to your beliefs" mean to you?

_____

_____

_____

2. How do you think personal superstitions might develop?

3. Considering the concepts of self-fulfilling prophecy and focusing, show how superstitions sometimes prove accurate.

_____

_____

_____

4. What are some of the advantages of being a passive waiter?

_____

_____

_____

5. Explain why the courage to be imperfect is so crucial to a person's development.

_____

_____

_____

6. Explain why people might resist new experiences in life.

_____

_____

_____

7. What is the crossroads approach to dealing with personal gripes and complaints?

8. What is the difference between calling environment a cause and calling environment an invitation to behavior?

9. Describe the relationship between beliefs, emotions, and behavior?

_____

_____

_____

10. Describe the aspects of this chapter with which you disagree.

_____

_____

_____

11. List the areas of this chapter that had meaning for you.

_____

_____

_____

12. Record how you can become more courageous as a result of reading this chapter.

    _____

    _____

    _____

Acting Courageously to Reach Your Goals

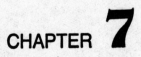

CHAPTER **7**

You are responsible for everything about yourself and your life! Your first responsibility is to decide what is real in your life and to accept it as fact. We suggest that you accept as reality anything you choose not to invest the time, money, and energy to change. When you do this, you overcome Error I (the error of disrespecting reality).

The second part of responsibility is to focus your energies enthusiastically in directions where you can have a reasonable amount of success. This involves, first of all, developing an identity as a complex, constantly growing person. This flowing identity suggests that you are always moving toward mastering new areas of your life, unhindered by "can'ts" or "this isn't me's." Next, we believe that to become courageous, you need to develop a greater self-respect. Self-respect is the feeling that "I am capable," "I am responsible," and "I am moving toward self-fulfillment." Only you can hold yourself back. We encouraged you to do a resource analysis of yourself by focusing on your positive resources—some you are aware of, some that are untapped (potential). Finally, to improve your relationship with yourself, we suggested energizing that powerful enthusiasm within to assist you in reaching your goals in life.

Courageous people speak in rational and responsible language. Chapter 5 discussed ways of enriching your language by eliminating "shoulds," "oughts," "musts," and "can'ts" from your speech. This chapter demonstrated the relationship between your language, your thinking, your emotions, and your behavior.

Chapter 6 discussed ways of overcoming discouraging fictional beliefs about yourself, other people, and the world. Courageous people are aware of the self-defeating fictions of their lives and constantly challenge these discouraging beliefs to help them achieve their goals. Each chapter presented attacking exercises for you to take fuller control of your life. The past six chapters were preparation for this chapter of action. Now your work and movement toward mastery goes into full swing.

We believe that you function as a whole, complete person. Consequently, as one aspect of your life changes—for example, your way of *thinking* about a problem—other aspects of your life tend to change also—for example, your *feelings*, your *language*, and your *actions* in dealing with the problem.

This means that as your language became more responsible, your feelings, your thinking, and your behavior also became more responsible. So, we trust that part of your movement toward self-mastery has already occurred.

At this point, we tend to agree with Glasser (1975) that ultimately the most important proof of your mastery involves changes in your *actions*. Developing your courage in feeling, speaking, and thinking assists your active movement toward achieving your goals. In this chapter you can put it all together into a courageous, holistic you—into a fuller life.

The Systematic Process of Self-Encouragement

ANALYZING YOUR PROBLEM

Your first task is to define your problem. In that process, consider a situation or situations in which you currently choose to lack courage. What changes would you ideally like to make? Do these changes involve changing your behaviors, changing your viewpoint, or changing someone else you believe is interfering with your reaching your goals? Talk to yourself for a few minutes to define the problem carefully. Be as specific as possible, and include any information that is relevant. Here is an example.

EXAMPLE PROBLEM
   My problem is that I would like to lose about fifteen pounds. I can't resist sweets.

Now define a problem you have had:

_____

_____

_____

REALISTIC POSITIVISM—DEVELOPING A COURAGEOUS PHILOSOPHY

Now that you have thought about and defined a problem you are facing, take a few minutes to review the philosophy of realistic positivism (Chapter 3). First, accept the fact that *you and no one else is responsible for your problems*. If someone else is inviting you to be discouraged, it is your responsibility either to change courageously or accept the limitation.

Ask yourself, "What part of my problem is real?" We have divided the aspects of the problem into universal realities (facts) and personal realities (observations). Here are some realistic components of the weight-loss problem that was previously mentioned.

EXAMPLE PROBLEM 1:
SOME REALISTIC COMPONENTS
1. If I continue to eat sweets, I will continue to gain weight. (*universal reality or facts*)

2. I have a craving for sweets. *(personal reality or personal observation)*

3. Unless I change my eating habits, I will not reach my goal of losing weight. *(universal reality or facts)*

4. If I want to achieve my goal, it will probably be effective for me to stop eating sweets. *(universal reality or facts)*

This individual has recognized the cause/effect nature of gaining weight, thereby facing reality head-on, but the individual has not fully taken responsibility, as reflected in Statement 2: "I have a craving for sweets." Why do we call this a shifting of responsibility? Well, saying "I have a craving for sweets" implies that the individual is helplessly being controlled by this "craving force." Although this appears to be personally real to him, it probably is not a fact. Perhaps he is treating an observation as a fact.

To avoid this error, be certain to take responsibility for your statements (Chapters 1 and 2). Remember—reality is never to blame when you do not reach your goals. Reality is neither for nor against you. Reality is just the way it is. It makes no compromises. Your frustration and discouragement are related to your belief that reality should be on your side. It is not the job of reality to understand you; it is your job to go 100 percent of the way to understanding the rules of reality.

Now look at your own defined problem again. Jot in as many realistic statements as you can about your problem.

EXPRESSED PROBLEM

_____

_____

_____

REALISTIC COMPONENTS (UNIVERSAL REALITIES
OR FACTS ABOUT MY PROBLEM)

_____

_____

_____

PERSONAL REALITIES (OBSERVATIONS ABOUT MY PROBLEM)

_____

_____

_____

Look again at your list—which statements fit into universal
reality, and which statements belong to your personal reality? You
have now de-Santa Claused yourself and are away ahead of most of
the four billion other people in the world. *You, unlike most people,
have faced reality!* This exercise addressed the first part of the
philosophy of realistic positivism—that is, reality. Near the end of
this chapter, we again discuss the second component of realistic
positivism—positivism—under the title "Perceptual Alternatives."

Building a Courageous
Relationship with Yourself

A FLOWING IDENTITY

In Chapter 4 we discussed ways of energizing that inner courage to enhance your relationship with yourself (intrapersonal). The
first important component of your intrapersonal relationship is to

develop a flowing, as opposed to a granitelike, personal identity. Again, consider the person who wanted to lose weight and felt overwhelmed by his craving for sweets.

GRANITELIKE IDENTITY	FLOWING IDENTITY
I'm the kind of person who has a craving for sweets. *I can't* quit eating sweets.	*In the past, I have noticed* that when there were sweets in the house, I would have a strong tendency to eat them. *If I change this tendency*, then in the future I will be the kind of person who is able to master a sweets craving.
I'm too heavy.	In my present state I am fifteen pounds overweight. If, however, I lose fifteen pounds, then I will not be overweight.
I'm not desirable. (Error: A personal observation made into a universal reality.)	*I believe* (making it what it is—a personal observation) that being fifteen pounds overweight makes me undesirable. So, if I lose fifteen pounds, maybe I would be more appealing to people.

When this person realizes that his weight is probably not stamped on him but is his responsibility either to change or to accept, he develops a new identity. The new identity suggests that because something has been true in the past, it does not mean that it must be true in the present. In the discussion on the pulling power of goals, we concluded that by changing an identity and seeking new goals, you mobilize all your feelings, thoughts, and actions in the directions that you choose.

Define your problems with both the granitelike identity and a flowing personal identity:

YOUR EXPRESSED PROBLEM:

_____

_____

_____

GRANITELIKE IDENTITY (THIS IS ME.) I'm the kind of person who	FLOWING IDENTITY (THIS WAS ME!) In the past I've observed that
_____	_____
_____	_____
_____	_____

How does this change your viewpoint of the problem?

_____

_____

_____

SELF-RESPECT

Besides developing a flowing identity, it is important for you to move toward greater self-respect. Self-respect is accepting personal responsibility for your life (internal as opposed to external sources). This is the realization that only you can choose how to live. You are responsible for being open to gather as much information as possible from other sources, but in the end only you own responsibility for your behavior.

Self-respect involves the feeling that you are capable enough to move toward self-fulfillment. It does not guarantee you will reach your goals, but it does guarantee that you can move toward them. We believe that movement toward those goals is in itself success. After all, if you never move toward your goals, how can you succeed? And if you keep moving toward them, you enhance the possibilities of reaching them. Consider some examples demonstrating the difference between personal disrespect and self-respect.

DISRESPECT IN SELF	SELF-RESPECT
Sure the world is flat. Everyone I know agrees with that.	It just does not make sense that the world is flat. I think it is round.
I know that if I try to cook that special dish of chicken for the family, I'll mess it up. So I'll play scared, and surely my mother will come in to rescue me.	I am determined to work at doing my best in cooking this meal. Perhaps I won't succeed this time—but it's my responsibility, and I'm not going to cop out. If I try enough, I'm sure to succeed.
All my friends smoke, and I feel out of place when I am with them if I do not smoke.	No, thank you. I don't want to smoke. (*Hidden message:* If our friendship is based upon something as tenuous as me smoking, that really is not a friendship.)

It has been said that one person with conviction is a majority. Self-respecting people are open to new ideas, but in the end they make up their own minds and take responsibility for their decisions without pointing the finger anywhere else. Consider some disrespectful and self-respectful statements you might make about your problems.

DISRESPECTFUL OF SELF (LEANING ON OTHERS)	SELF-RESPECTFUL (TAKING PERSONAL RESPONSIBILITY)
_____	_____
_____	_____
_____	_____

FOCUSING ON YOUR RESOURCES

Focusing involves emphasizing certain aspects of yourself and deemphasizing others. Courageous people have a talent for focusing on their perceived strengths, assets, and resources. Discouraged people focus on their perceived weaknesses.

Your mind is powerful. It is unlimited in its potential. At this moment you can remember some of the best, most courageous moments of your lifetime. You can grow from these moments. You can realize that on these occasions, it was your courage and your strengths that helped you reach your goals.

In *Turning People On* (1977) we discussed the importance of claims-to-fame. Claims-to-fame are proud moments in your life that were meaningful to you, though perhaps the rest of the world couldn't have cared less. These are some of the many claims-to-fame we have heard:

Rachel was always good at spelling. She won many spelling contests as she went through school.

Danny has a real talent for solving math problems.

Tom is in excellent physical shape. At the age of thirty-two, he can run a five-minute mile.

Judy is a talented dancer.

What are some of your claims-to-fame?

_____

_____

_____

By focusing on your claims-to-fame, positive points, assets, and resources, you are putting your best foot forward. Courage involves energizing all your assets to deal with life and to reach your goals most effectively.

Your assets are tools that can work for you. The more you have, the more likely it is you will reach your goals. Refer to Chapter 4 where you completed an asset analysis. Again record your assets below. Add any additional ones you feel at this moment:

_____

_____

_____

Refer also to the potentiality analysis you completed in Chapter 4. A potentiality analysis is composed of those aspects of yourself that you currently consider liabilities but that could be turned into assets. Record your previous responses as well as any additional potentialities you feel at the present time.

_____

_____

_____

These are just a *fraction* of your total assets, resources, and potentialities. Constantly keep them in mind. These are your tools—and it is difficult to construct a more positive life without tools. Record below any additional assets, strengths, or resources that you want to develop in the future.

_____

_____

_____

Along with focusing, become aware of your assets, liabilities, self-talk. Work at rerouting liability talk. Shortly, we discuss ways of turning liability talk into constructive growth or task involvement.

> Your resources are tools that can work for you—if you take them out of your toolbox to construct a more productive you.

DEVELOPING YOUR ENTHUSIASM

Your enthusiasm is the energy that propels you to your successes. Enthusiasm, combined with your flowing identity, self-respect, and especially your resources, is unbeatable. The only price you pay for this combination is hard work and constant positive focusing.

As we said before, this is your moment in the history of the universe. What do you want? How many more of your 25,600 days are going to pass before you move enthusiastically toward your goals?

Develop your goals, and be pulled by them. Turn on your enthusiasm, and go. Refer to the chart in Chapter 4 that contrasts the discouraging outlook with the encouraging, enthusiastic view-point on life.

Develop a plan to keep yourself enthusiastic. What other feel-ings, thoughts, or actions could you include in this list that turn you on? Constantly focus on them:

_____

_____

_____

Remember, this all came from inside you—it was already there. All you had to do was bring it out. And there is much more there!

Another way of speaking courageously is to be sensitive to the use of the word *can't*. We believe that "can't" is one of the most overused words in the English language. "Can't" gives you permis-sion not to grow. Examine whether your "can'ts" are really "won'ts." *Won't* is a much more responsible word.

We suggested eliminating "shoulds," "oughts," and "musts" from your vocabulary. These three words are not facts. They are human inventions and serve no positive purpose in the vocabulary of courageous people. They also are the source of anger, depression, guilt, and many other self-defeating emotions. Instead of using "should," "ought," and "must," Albert Ellis suggested that you select more rational talk. These three words reflect personal gran-diosity. More rational alternatives to these words include "I would prefer if . . . " or "if I could choose, I would choose this" or "if this were an issue that was on the ballot, I would vote this way." These three phrases are sane and help you keep in touch with your perspective on the universe.

We encouraged you to be sensitive to using words that tend to catastrophize events. The words *horrible, awful, terrible,* and *devas-*

tating are just a few examples of words with connotations that tend to cripple your ability to cope rationally and effectively. Perhaps such words as *inconvenient, unfortunate,* and *nuts* might be more appropriate.

Listen to the language of people. You will probably notice that those who seem to have a greater ability to deal with stress speak more courageously. Words give you clues as to how you could view a situation. Give yourself only constructive clues.

Developing Courageous Beliefs

Your beliefs or your outlook on life affects the way you feel and the way you choose to act. We discussed in Chapter 3 that it is the way you view life—not the circumstances of your life—that ultimately affects you. To support this, think about two of your friends—one who panics at the least amount of stress and one who seems able to handle much frustration. Imagine how each would cope with these circumstances:

- loss of a loved one
- winning a million dollars
- being fired.

If you imagined each person reacting differently to the same event, you understand how a person's beliefs—not the external circumstances—are what eventually affect emotional adjustment.

Chapter 6 discussed some possible discouraging fictional beliefs about yourself, other people, and the world. When you suffer from the magical fiction, you believe that there is magic in the world to help you reach your goals without full effort on your part. Can you think of times when you dodged a responsibility, feeling that there was magic to help you?

The perfectionistic fiction is the belief that unless you're perfect, you're worthless. This fiction can be discouraging when you stop trying out of fear of failure. In what areas of your life are you a perfectionist? Is it a constructive perfectionism, or is it defensive perfectionism? Defensive perfectionists are working from weaknesses rather than strengths.

Complaining and blaming fictions were also discussed in Chapter 6. We encouraged you to think about the fictions in your life. Consider reading A New Guide to Rational Living by Ellis and Harper (1975) for a more detailed discussion on discouraging fictions.

Ellis and Harper detail ten false assumptions in A New Guide to Rational Living. These are similar to the discouraging fictions discussed here. The ten false assumptions or irrational ideas include:

1. I must have love and approval from all of the people I find significant.

2. I must prove to be thoroughly competent and achieving in whatever I do.

3. When people act obnoxiously or unfairly they are bad, wicked or rotten.

4. I must view things as awful, terrible or horrible when I'm treated unfairly or rejected.

5. Emotional misery comes from external pressure and I have no control of it.

6. If something seems dangerous or fearsome, I must preoccupy myself with thinking about it.

7. It is easier to avoid life's problems than to face them.

8. My past must continue to control me today.

9. Events in my life should turn out better than they do.

10. I can achieve happiness by sitting back passively.

In this chapter we have reviewed ways of improving your relationship with yourself, developing courageous language, and overcoming discouraging fictions about yourself, other people, and the world. You are a whole, complete person. Keep in mind all these aspects of yourself. Now move toward those goals.

Courageous Action

ENCOURAGING YOURSELF

You are your own best friend or worst enemy—which one is your choice. You evaluate yourself and your actions. As you gain self-respect, you conclude that in the end, it is you who are responsible for your decision. How does this personal evaluation take place within you? What goes on when you are drawing conclusions about yourself?

We believe that despite your complexity, it is possible to develop helpful ways of understanding how you judge yourself. One helpful distinction was developed by William James (1963) years ago. James addressed two components of the person—the "I" and the "me." We believe that self-encouragement involves developing an awareness of both aspects. It also involves teaching your "I" to be a more effective empathizer and encourager of your "me."

What or who are your "I" and "me"? We will answer this question with a question: Have you ever talked to yourself about yourself? Have you ever found yourself observing yourself? These are some statements that demonstrate this intrapersonal activity.

I: Boy, what a fool I made out of myself last night at the party.

I: I'm really annoyed with my mother-in-law. She is so pushy. I think she can tell I'm angry at her by the way I'm acting.

I: I look pretty darn good in this new dress.

These comments demonstrate that a part of you is evaluating your feelings, thoughts, or actions. We call this evaluator the "I" of you. The feelings, thoughts, or behavior that the "I" is observing is the "me." So "I" observe and evaluate "me." Write in some statements and observations that your "I" makes of your "me":

I: _____

I: _____

I: _____

Your "me" is the actor or performer, and your "I" is the critic in the audience. Your "me" desperately needs the encouragement of your "I." Since both these hypothetical components exist within you, what your "I" tells your "me" can be either self-encouraging or self-discouraging.

In your statements, did you find that your "I" tended to be encouraging or discouraging in its comments about your "me"? Consider the following list, which describes the functions and activities of your "I" and your "me."

"I"	"ME"
Knower	Known
Evaluator, criticizer	Performer

WHEN YOUR "I" . . .	YOUR "ME"
Discourages	Gives up, defends
Encourages	Tries harder, grows
Focuses on weaknesses	Loses self-esteem, feels incapable
Focuses on strengths	Feels capable

Your "I," then, is similar to the teacher, as it constantly evaluates your "me." But at least you can get away from the critical teacher at the end of the school year. A negatively critical and discouraging "I" remains with you until you stop accepting the invitation to be discouraged.

Your "I" can be your best friend or worst enemy. Equip your "I" with all your strengths, assets, and resources. Let it be your best encourager. Since your "I" is always with you, it's the best friend you can have.

ENCOURAGING "I"

OK — YOU FAILED AT THAT TASK — ANALYZE IT, AND TRY AGAIN.

YOUR WORTH AS A PERSON IS
NOT BASED ON YOUR PERFORMANCE

Your "I" can discourage your "me" when it tends to equate your worth with the performance of your "me." There is no proof that your worth is greater when you earn an A grade than when you earn a D. If this were so, then your human worth would shift like the Dow Jones average. In *Humanistic Psychotherapy* (1973), Ellis comments:

> A basic tenet for rational living is that people not rate themselves in terms of any of their performances, but instead fully accept themselves in terms of their being, their existence. Otherwise, they tend to be severely self-deprecating and insecure, and as a consequence they function ineffectively.
>
> Why should this be so? To value oneself in terms of any deeds or acts will work only as long as one is performing well. Even if such deeds or acts are excellent at the moment, it will probably be only a matter of time when they will become less praiseworthy. [p. 17]

We believe that it is much more encouraging to rate your talents rather than your worth as a person. Rating your skills is not only more encouraging; it is also more accurate. Consider the following differences.

RATING WORTH AS A PERSON	RATING SKILLS, TALENTS, PERFORMANCE
John is a *good* person.	John is a *skilled* mechanic.
Mary shoveled our snow. She is such a *nice* person.	Mary shoveled our snow. We appreciated that. It was *helpful* to us.
I am a *worthless* person. Everything I do turns out wrong.	I am currently *lacking skills* in dancing and singing.
I am a *stupid* person.	On that spelling test today, I *had two out of fifteen correctly spelled*.

Rating your worth or that of someone else as a human being is an overgeneralization and thus is unsupported. Concerning psychotherapeutic approaches, Ellis (1973) wrote:

The more elegant approach is to show the individual that he does not have to rate, assess or value himself at all; that he can merely accept the fact that he exists; that it is better for him to live and enjoy than for him to die or be in pain; and that he can take more delight in living by only measuring and valuing his traits, characteristics and performance than by superfluously bothering to value his so-called self. Once the client is helped to be fully tolerant of all humans, including yourself, and to stop giving them any global report cards, he has a philosophic solution to the problems of personal worth and can truly be self-accepting rather than self-evaluating. He will then consider himself neither a good nor a bad human being, but a person with fortunate and unfortunate traits. He will truly accept his humanity and stop demanding superhumanness from anyone. [pp. 28–29]

We agree with Ellis. When your "I" focuses on your effort, skills, and performance rather than on your worth as a person, your "me" can become more task-involved than ego-involved.

EGO-INVOLVEMENT VERSUS TASK-INVOLVEMENT

When you are ego-involved in a situation, you are concerned with your ego or your own worth as a person. Ego-involvement frequently interferes with your growth and problem solving. Remember our friend (the self-blamer) who was rejected? Our friend has coped in an ego-involved way, and we see the use of exaggerated language. His energies are being directed to blaming, and he is talking himself into a deeper and deeper rut. The rut, remember, will protect him temporarily, since if he does not ask anyone else to go out, he need not fear being rejected again. This is typical of many people when they are ego-involved. Their energies are being spent, not constructively in solving their problems, but rather in patching up their egos. The more ego-involved people are, the more

SELF-BLAMER

SELF-RESPONSIBLE PERSON

likely it is they see only one way of responding to invited stress. They become blamers and feel they *automatically* must become depressed by rejection. They feel they had no choice in the matter (S→R).

1. THERE ARE MANY OTHER GIRLS TO ASK OUT, OR

2. I AM GOING TO TRY AGAIN, PERHAPS BY ASKING HER WHAT SHE WOULD LIKE TO DO AT THIS TIME.

Now our other friend experienced the same rejection. Remember, it is the same *stimulus*. The same stimulus but different responses—why? Because this individual was task-involved. His energies were directed to developing improved skills and problem-solving abilities, not ego patching. He was more aware of the possible numer of ways to respond. He was, then, more fully aware of the "you" in the S→You→R! Again, the more task-involved you are, the more you recognize your role in creating a blameless, effective response that is constructive. Your energies are not directed to maintaining your ego but rather are creatively involved in searching for the best response. Look at a comparison of ego-involvement with task-involvement.

EGO-INVOLVED S→R	TASK-INVOLVED S→You→R
How do I look?	What is the best answer? I'll experiment—see what happens.
If it doesn't work out, I couldn't stand it.	If it doesn't work out, there must be a better way.
Only one answer.	Many answers.
Panics when wrong.	Learns from errors to improve future behavior.
Closed-mindedness.	Open-mindedness.
Must have own way.	Looks for the best way. If someone else's way is more effective, then that way is more appropriate.

Choose a past situation in which you responded in an ego-involved way. How could have you been more task-involved?

_____

_____

_____

Is there a situation in the near future where you will feel invited to be ego-involved? If so, how can you prepare yourself to cope in a more task-involved manner?

_____

_____

_____

DEFINING YOUR GOALS AND MOVEMENT

What is your ultimate goal for your 25,600 days? Again, if this is not accomplished by you—who will do it? How much do you want this and other goals? Take out a piece of paper, and write (in big print) your ultimate goal and when you want to achieve it. Include a time, a day, and a year. Hang this paper on your wall or in a place where you spend a lot of time and where you feel comfortable. Record your ultimate goal below:

_____

_____

_____

On another piece of paper, write this sentence: "I, and only I, am responsible to reach my goal." Remember, in Chapter 3, "Realistic Positivism," we discussed the importance of respecting reality. It is crucial to understand and accept what is real and could provide a barrier. When you understand and face reality, you can make it work for you. When you fight reality, it resists, and you waste your valuable energies in directions other than your stated goals.

Remember, *you are the responsible one*. You may encounter much resistance. You are not responsible for the resistances that reality puts in your way—but you are responsible for overcoming them. *But overcoming resistances is part of the fun and part of the feeling of mastery that you will eventually experience.* After all, it's no fun winning a game of checkers or chess if you have played by yourself. Your two opponents are, in this order, yourself and reality.

REACHING YOUR GOALS:
YOU VERSUS YOU

You are your chief opponent. If your "I" discourages your "me," you can talk yourself out of your goals. This sort of self-talk discouragement is the most destructive, because your "I" is constantly with you. We suggest that you decide to *fire your discouraging, ego-involved "I" at this moment*. To show your discouraging "I" that you can see right through it, jot in some comments it would have told your "me" to interfere with your stated goals; for example, "You dummy, you will never reach this goal—who are you kidding?" Record below comments that your discouraging "I" would have made before it was fired:

_____

_____

_____

Your discouraging "I" is a product of your unrealized goals. In Chapter 2 we discussed Assumption II: "All your feelings, thoughts, and actions are pulled by your goals." We said:

Although you are the executive of all your feelings, thoughts, and actions, most of the time you fail to make your goals clear. And when you fail to develop clear goals, other unrealized goals may take over. Remember that your feelings, thoughts, and actions are constantly being pulled by either your stated goals or your unrealized goals.

Your unrealized goals are a tough opponent. Short-term satisfaction, blaming, giving up, and making excuses are symptoms of unrealized goals. Remember, all your energies are going to be devoted to your stated or your unrealized goals. Observe again the example of this struggle that Ethel faced between the unrealized goals and the stated goals in Chapter 2.

Defining Your Movement toward Your Goals

You have now fired your discouraging "I." Renew your contract with your encouraging "I." You have stated one or perhaps more than one long-range goal. This, of course, is the ideal. At this point encourage yourself to state some immediate goals that you are confident are reachable over the short range. We suggest that these goals be in the direction of the ideal goal. For example:

IDEAL LONG-RANGE STATED GOAL

I want to earn a college degree and become an outstanding teacher by _____

SHORT-RANGE GOAL

I will go to visit a college and talk to the counselor at the school about their program and admission requirements. I will do this tomorrow at 10:00 A.M.

A long-range stated goal is nothing more than a series of short-range goals. It is crucial to include the following in all your goals:

1. *Clarify your goal; be specific, not vague.* For example, "I want self-confidence" is too vague. Perhaps "I want to be able to make an appointment for admission at the college." Specific goals are observable and thus avoid what the discouraging "I" loves—vagueness and loopholes.

2. *Whenever possible, state a time, date, place, etc.*

3. *Have at least one short-range goal each day.* Give yourself a reason to get up early the next morning.

4. *Think about how your feelings, thoughts, and actions can be pulled by your stated goal.*

5. *Recognize and attack the resistances put forth by your unrealized goals.*

6. *Keep focusing on your goal and the next step in reaching it, the movement toward the goal, not just on success or failure.*

7. *Feel that sense of mastery every time you make even the smallest step in the direction of your goal.*

ACCEPT NO EXCUSES, NO BLAME

Tolerate no excuse in the movement toward your goals. As a human being, you are quite talented at rationalizing, justifying, and excusing. This is counterproductive and reflects the blaming fringe benefits discussed in Chapter 1. We are way beyond that at this point. William Glasser (1973) comments on excuses in *Reality Therapy*:

> Plans fail sometimes, but the reality therapist makes it clear to the patient that excuses are unacceptable. When the patient explains that a particular plan failed, it has been our experience that little therapeutic gain occurs from exploring whether the plan failed for a valid reason. (p. 303)

Whenever you find yourself justifying or excusing, stop and regroup. Ask yourself, "Do I still want to achieve my goal? When will I start up again? What can I do to avoid this last pitfall (if it is still appropriate)?"

Blaming is unhelpful, primitive, and counterproductive. Also destructive is self-punishment, as Glasser points out: Never punish yourself—it takes too much time and is a product of your unrealized goals. Instead, decide whether you want to continue to seek your goal, and reorganize your steps. *Most importantly, keep moving!*

Perceptual Alternatives

USING THE POWER OF YOUR MIND TO REACH YOUR GOALS

Perceptual alternatives, you will recall from Chapter 3, are all the alternative ways of viewing your life or a specific situation. When you are stuck for goals or for specific approaches to reaching them, reread the part of Chapter 3 on perceptual alternatives, and brainstorm many, many plans.

Your mind is your most powerful asset. At first, jot down any possibility without evaluating whether it is good or bad. The universe is the limit—no boundaries. After spending considerable time, couple these alternatives with those assets, resources, talents, and strengths that you have listed in Chapter 4 and previously in this chapter. Remember, self-encouragement involves focusing on your positive components. Develop or redevelop your plan and goals. So when you are invited again to become discouraged, remember:

1. Avoid excusing, blaming, and punishing yourself.

2. Keep in mind the self-fulfilling prophecy. If you believe you can, you can.

3. Keep respecting yourself and your opinions; yet remain open-minded to new sources of information.

4. Your past is past—develop that flowing identity.

5. Remember your complexity and all the unlimited possibilities you have. Remember the concept of perceptual alternatives.

6. Keep focusing on your strengths, assets, resources, and possibilities.

7. Keep your enthusiasm high.

8. Watch your language; avoid self-defeating talk such as "can'ts," passive language, and blaming language.

9. Recognize that it is the way you look at a situation—not the way a situation is—that ultimately affects you.

10. Constantly combat your discouraging fictional beliefs— magic, perfection, blaming, complaining, etc.

11. Recognize reality and your perspective in the universe. De-Santa Claus yourself; you are one of four billion, although perhaps you are a rare one, because of your courage.

And finally, remember:

I am responsible for everything about me and my life.

Thus I was responsible for this personal growth that I have made and will continue to make for the remainder of my 25,600 days.

Me plus my courage equals one dynamite person!

References

Ansbacher, H., & R. Ansbacher. *The Individual Psychology of Alfred Adler.* New York: Basic Books, 1956.

Dinkmeyer, D., *The Basics of Self-acceptance.* Coral Springs, Fla.: CMTI Press, 1977.

Dinkmeyer, D., & L. Losoncy. *The Encouragement Book.* Englewood Cliffs, N.J.: Prentice-Hall, in press.

Ellis, A. *Reason and Emotion in Psychotherapy.* New York: Lyle Stuart, 1962.

Ellis, A. *Humanistic Psychotherapy.* New York: McGraw-Hill, 1973.

Ellis, A., & R. Harper. *A New Guide to Rational Living.* North Hollywood, Calif.: Wilshire Book Company, 1975.

Frankl, V. *Man's Search for Meaning.* Boston: Beacon Press, 1959.

Glasser, W. *Reality Therapy.* New York: Harper & Row, 1975.

Glasser, W., & L. M. Zunin. "Reality Therapy." In R. Corsini (Ed.), *Current Psychotherapies.* Itasca, Ill.: F. E. Peacock Publishers, 1973.

James, W. *Principles of Psychology.* New York: Fawcett Books Group—CBS Publications, 1963.

Lazarus, A., & A. Fay. *I Can If I Want to.* New York: Morrow, 1975.

Losoncy, L. *Turning People On.* Englewood Cliffs, N.J.: Prentice-Hall, 1977.

Maslow, A. *Motivation and Personality.* New York: Harper & Row, 1954.

May, R. *Love and Will.* New York: Norton, 1969.

O'Connell, W., & M. Bright. *The Natural High Primer.* Chicago: Alfred Adler Institute, 1977.

Powers, R. L., & J. M. Hahn, "Resignation or Courage: The Wisdom to See the Difference." *Personnel and Guidance Journal,* 1978, 57 (4), 219–220.

Rogers, C. R. *On Becoming a Person.* Boston: Houghton-Mifflin, 1961.

Skinner, B. F. *About Behaviorism.* New York: Knopf, 1973.

Zastrow, C. *Talk to Yourself.* Englewood Cliffs, N.J.: Prentice-Hall, 1979.